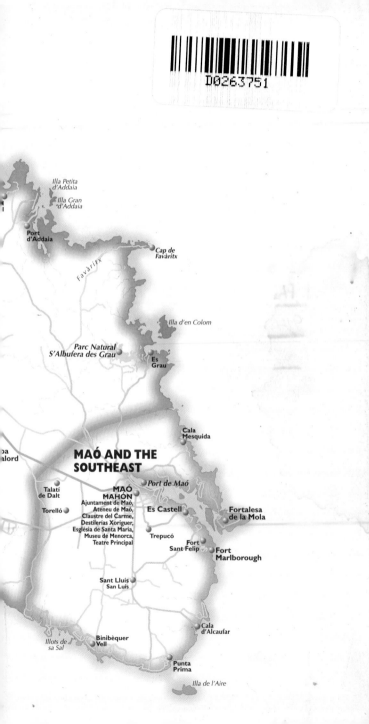

TWINPACK
Menorca

TONY KELLY

If you have any comments
or suggestions for this guide
you can contact the editor at
Twinpacks@theAA.com

AA Publishing
Find out more about AA Publishing and the wide
range of services the AA provides by visiting our
website at theAA.com/bookshop

How to Use This Book

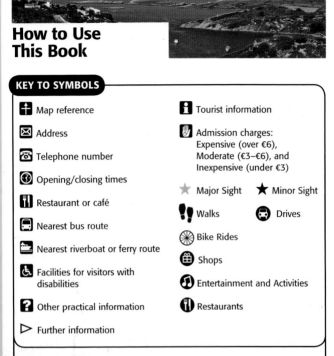

KEY TO SYMBOLS

➕ Map reference

✉ Address

☎ Telephone number

🕐 Opening/closing times

🍴 Restaurant or café

🚌 Nearest bus route

🚢 Nearest riverboat or ferry route

♿ Facilities for visitors with disabilities

❓ Other practical information

▷ Further information

ℹ Tourist information

✋ Admission charges: Expensive (over €6), Moderate (€3–€6), and Inexpensive (under €3)

★ Major Sight   ★ Minor Sight

👣 Walks   🚗 Drives

🚲 Bike Rides

🏢 Shops

🎭 Entertainment and Activities

🍴 Restaurants

This guide is divided into four sections

• Essential Menorca: An introduction to the island and tips on making the most of your stay.

• Menorca by Area: We've broken the island into four areas, and recommended the best sights, shops, entertainment venues, activities, nightlife and restaurants in each one. Suggested walks, a driving tour and a bike ride help you to explore the island.

• Where to Stay: The best hotels, whether you're looking for luxury, budget or something in between.

• Need to Know: The info you need to make your trip run smoothly, including getting about by public transport, weather tips, emergency phone numbers and useful websites.

Navigation In the Menorca by Area chapter, we've given each area its own colour, which is also used on the locator maps throughout the book and the map on the inside front cover.

Maps The fold-out map accompanying this book is a comprehensive map of Menorca. The grid on this fold-out map is the same as the grid on the locator maps within the book. The grid references to these maps are shown with capital letters, for example A1. The grid references to the town plan are shown with lower-case letters, for example a1.

Contents

CONTENTS

Introducing Menorca

Menorca is the quiet one of the Balearic islands. Mallorca may be bigger, Ibiza may be louder, but of all the Spanish islands, Menorca is the one that has managed to adapt to tourism without selling its soul.

Tourism is the driving force of the island's economy but Menorca's status as a UNESCO Biosphere Reserve ensures that it is committed to sustainable tourism alongside environmental protection and economic development. The building of high-rise hotels is strictly limited and most of the island's beaches are totally untouched. To reach them you may have to drive along a country lane then walk along the cliffs, but the experience is all the more rewarding as a result.

Inland is a bucolic countryside of meadows, stone walls and carved olive-wood gates, with cattle and sheep farming and a significant cheesemaking industry. Scattered among the fields are hundreds of megalithic monuments, remains of the Talaiotic culture which thrived on Menorca 3,000 years ago. The massive stone *talaiots* (watchtowers), *taulas* (T-shaped altars) and *navetas* (burial chambers) provide an enduring mystery and a fascinating link with the ancient world.

The cities at either end of the island face out to sea, as if deliberately turning their backs on one another. Ciutadella, the old Arab and Catalan capital, is a handsome town of noble palaces around a Gothic cathedral. Maó, with its elegant Georgian architecture, is largely a creation of Menorca's 18th-century British rulers, who moved the capital here to take advantage of its splendid natural harbour.

Menorca is changing, but only slowly. Restaurants serve new-wave fusion cuisine and boutique hotels are appearing, but unlike other Balearic islands, Menorca has no need to chase the latest trends. Its appeal is the same as it has ever been—a peaceful island of blue skies, golden sands and a relaxed Mediterranean lifestyle.

Facts + Figures

- **Population: 92,434**
- **Language: Menorquín, a dialect of Catalan. Spanish is also spoken.**
- **Number of beaches: 104**
- **Highest point: Monte Toro (▷ 54)**

THE BRITISH CONNECTION

The British ruled Menorca on and off for 71 years between 1708 and 1802. The influence of British rule remains today and includes Georgian architecture, Chippendale furniture, cricket, gin and words in the Menorquín dialect such as *grevi* (gravy) and *boinder* (bow-window).

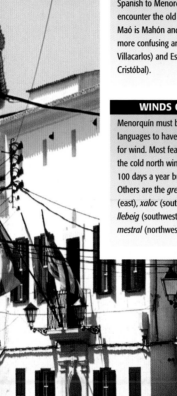

WHAT'S IN A NAME?

In recent years, maps and street signs have been rewritten to reflect the change from Spanish to Menorquín, but you may still encounter the old versions. In Spanish, Maó is Mahón and Ciutadella is Ciudadela; more confusing are Es Castell (formerly Villacarlos) and Es Migjorn Gran (San Cristóbal).

WINDS OF MENORCA

Menorquín must be one of the few languages to have eight different words for wind. Most feared is the *tramuntana*, the cold north wind that blows for over 100 days a year but is strongest in winter. Others are the *gregal* (northeast), *llevant* (east), *xaloc* (southeast), *migjorn* (south), *llebeig* (southwest), *ponent* (west) and *mestral* (northwest).

A Short Stay in Menorca

DAY 1: MAÓ

Morning Start your day with coffee on Plaça de S'Esplanada in Maó. The former parade ground, with a British-built barracks at one end, is now a leafy main square with terrace cafés, benches and a children's playground. A market is held here on Tuesday and Saturday mornings.

Mid-morning Visit the **Museu de Menorca** (▷ 30) for a quick overview of Menorcan history, then stroll downhill to **Església de Santa Maria** (▷ 36) in time for the organ recital at 11am. Afterwards, head for the covered market at **Claustre del Carme** (▷ 35) to stock up on delicious Mahón cheese.

Lunch Take the steps down to the harbour for lunch by the water—**Varadero** (▷ 44) specializes in paella and seafood.

Afternoon Take a cruise around **Port de Maó** (▷ 32) with Yellow Catamarans, soaking up the sunshine on the top deck and enjoying views of Maó up on the cliff.

Early evening Follow the promenade to Cala Figuera, admiring the yachts moored in the harbour, for a drink at one of the seafront bars. If you want to stay here for the evening, numerous restaurants on Moll de Llevant offer everything from pizza to fresh fish.

Dinner Take a taxi to **Es Castell** (▷ 24) for dinner by the harbourside at Cales Fonts. You can take your pick of the waterfront restaurants, but **Vell Parrander** (▷ 44) is a good choice.

Evening Finish your day with a drink in **Es Cau** (▷ 42), listening to Spanish folk songs and guitars in an atmospheric cave bar at Cala Corb.

DAY 2: CIUTADELLA

Morning Head across the island to spend your second day in **Ciutadella** (▷ 90). Buses from Maó stop in Plaça dels Pins, close to Plaça des Born. You can easily spend all morning wandering the narrow streets of the old town, visiting the **Catedral de Menorca** (▷ 97) and **Museu Diocesà de Menorca** (▷ 98).

Mid-morning Take a break from sightseeing and indulge in a spot of people-watching from a seat at Es Quiosc, an open-air café in the heart of Plaça des Born. Alternatively, have coffee at **Cercle Artístic** (▷ 103), a historic 19th-century coffee house on the square.

Lunch You don't have to go far for the best view in Ciutadella. Arrive early to get a table on the balcony at **Ca's Cònsol** (▷ 105), with views over the harbour as you dine.

Afternoon Time to head for the beach. Ciutadella has its own small beach at Cala d'es Degollador, or you can take a bus to **Cala Blanca** (▷ 99) or drive to **Cala Macarella** (▷ 74).

Early evening Join the locals for their promenade along the Passeig Marítim, enjoying the views of Mallorca as the sun sets over the sea from **Castell de Sant Nicolau** (▷ 97).

Dinner It's hard to beat either the setting or the seafood at **Café Balear** (▷ 105), with tables on the waterfront right by the port.

Evening If you still have some energy, it is just a short stroll to Pla de Sant Joan, an open space behind the harbour whose terrace clubs and bars are packed until early morning in summer (▷ 103).

Top 25

▶ ▶ ▶

Binisues ▷ 72 Manor house, natural science collection and museum of antique farm tools.

Cala del Pilar ▷ 73 Walk through the oak and pine woods to reach a remote sandy bay.

Cala Macarella ▷ 74 Is this Menorca's most beautiful beach? Decide for yourself.

Torre d'en Galmés ▷ **60** A good introduction to Menorca's megalithic monuments, which is easily accessible to wheelchairs and pushchairs.

Torralba d'en Salord ▷ **59** Well-preserved and clearly explained Talaiotic village near Alaior.

Teatre Principal ▷ 34 Restored opera house in Maó with performances throughout the year.

Son Catlar ▷ 96 Largest surviving prehistoric site on Menorca, still surrounded by its ancient walls and set in peaceful surroundings.

Son Bou ▷ 58 Sun, sea and sand on Menorca's longest beach where the ancient meets the modern.

Port de Maó ▷ 32 Cruise around the world's second-longest natural harbour and watch history unfold on the shore.

Map labels:

Illes Bledes

Cala del Pilar

CIUTADELLA AND THE WEST 87–106

WESTERN CENTRAL MENORCA 69–86

Castell Santa Águeda

Pedreres de S'Hostal

Naveta des Tudons

Binisues

Ciutadella de Menorca

Hort de Sant Patrici

Son Catlar

Artrutx

Cala Macarella

Cala Santa Galdana

Pedreres de S'Hostal ▷ **94** A disused quarry ingeniously turned into a work of art.

Parc Natural S'Albufera des Grau ▷ **56** Wetland nature reserve with easy lakeside walks.

Naveta des Tudons ▷ **92** Fascinating Bronze Age burial chamber in the countryside near Ciutadella.

These pages are a quick guide to the Top 25, which are described in more detail later. Here they are listed alphabetically, and the tinted background shows which area they are in.

Cala Santa Galdana
▷ **76** Bustling resort set around a fabulous horse-shoe bay.

Cales Coves ▷ **48** Ancient cave necropolis carved into the rocks at these twin coves.

Cap de Cavalleria ▷ **49** Wild and lonely landscape on the north coast with a long human history.

Es Castell ▷ **24** Harbourside garrison town with British colonial architecture.

Castell Santa Àgueda ▷ **78** Ruined Moorish castle with great views.

Ciutadella ▷ **90** Gothic palaces and churches in Menorca's stately former capital.

Fornells ▷ **50** A picturesque Mediterranean fishing village.

Fortalesa de la Mola ▷ **26** Abandoned fort at the entrance to Maó harbour, home to the largest gun ever built in Spain.

Fort Marlborough ▷ **28** Explore the secret tunnels of an 18th-century fortress.

Hort de Sant Patrici ▷ **79** Farmhouse museum dedicated to Mahón cheese with free samples to taste.

Illa de Sanitja o dels Porros
Cap de Cavalleria

Fornells
Badia de Fornells

EASTERN CENTRAL MENORCA 45-68

Illa Petita d'Addaia
Illa Gran d'Addaia

Es Mercadal 357
Monte Toro

Favàritx

Illa d'en Colom

Parc Natural S'Albufera des Grau

Torre d'en Galmés *Torralba d'en Salord*

MAÓ AND THE SOUTHEAST 20-44

MAÓ MAHÓN *Port de Maó*
Museu de Menorca, Teatre Principal *Es Castell* *Fortalesa de la Mola*

Cales Coves

Penyes d'Alaior

Fort Marlborough

Illots de sa Sal

Illa de l'Aire

Museu de Menorca
▷ **30** The best place to learn about Menorca's long and varied history.

Monte Toro ▷ **54** Hilltop pilgrimage chapel of local legend with stunning views across the island.

Es Mercadal ▷ **52** Market town in the heart of the island known for its crafts and cuisine.

◀ ◀ ◀

Beaches

It may be a small island but Menorca has over 100 beaches, from long stretches of golden sand to tiny bays and coves with room for a handful of towels. Some of the more popular beaches can get crowded in July and August, but even then it only takes a little effort to get off the beaten track and discover your own unspoiled beach.

Beach resorts

Official maps of Menorca's beaches divide them into three categories, beginning with those situated in urban areas and tourist resorts. Examples include Son Bou, Sant Tomàs, Cala Santa Galdana, Cala En Porter and Arenal d'en Castell. These beaches have facilities including sun loungers and parasols for hire, pedal boats, watersports, restaurants and bars. They are also accessible by public transport. In 2009, nine of Menorca's beaches were awarded the Blue Flag for cleanliness, safety and environmental awareness. They included seven beaches around Ciutadella (Sa Caleta d'en Gorries, Cala En Blanes, Sa Caleta, Cala Santandría, Cala Blanca, Cala En Bosc and Son Xoriguer) plus Cala Santa Galdana and Son Bou.

Virgin beaches

The second category of beaches are those with limited or no facilities, but which are accessible by road. Examples include some of the most beautiful beaches on the island at Cala d'Algaiarens, Cala En Turqueta and Cala Macarella. These 'virgin' beaches have benefitted in recent years from a government

From rocky coves to wide sandy beaches–there are endless opportunities to enjoy Menorca's coastline

---

NATURISM

Although there are no official nudist beaches on Menorca, naturism is tolerated away from the large beach resorts. Popular beaches for naturists include Cala Macarelleta, Cala Mitjana, Binigaus and the western end of Son Bou. In practice, it is acceptable to strip off at any of the more remote beaches, such as Cala d'Algaiarens and Cala del Pilar. Topless sunbathing is acceptable everywhere.

campaign to buy up farmland behind the coast in order to provide free access—until recently you had to cross private land and pay a toll to get there. Some of these beaches are now so popular in summer that electronic boards have been erected on the Ciutadella ring road warning drivers when the parking areas are full. Leave your car and walk down to the beach, in some cases a 20-minute walk.

Secret coves
If you really want to get away from it all, head for one of the 52 remote beaches which are accessible only on foot or by boat. Examples include Cala del Pilar, Cala Trebalúger and Cala Tortuga. Some of these can be reached on the Camí de Cavalls, a 17th-century bridle path around the entire Menorcan coast which was once used for military purposes. The path has gradually fallen into disuse, but is now being restored by the island government and several sections are open and marked with wooden arrows. Needless to say, there are no facilities at these beaches, so take a picnic and plenty of water and take all your rubbish away with you.

Protecting the beaches
Menorca's coastline is a fragile resource which needs to be preserved for future generations. As a visitor to the island you can help by always using the designated car parking areas, making sure that you do not disturb wildlife or plants and by being careful to avoid walking on sand dunes and other vulnerable areas.

SAFETY FLAGS

During the peak season from June to September, the larger beaches are patrolled by lifeguards who operate a coded system of flags warning you when it is safe to swim.

● Red flag: Do not go into the sea.
● Yellow flag: Take care. Confident swimmers may enter the sea but children should stay out of the water.
● Green flag: It is safe to swim.

Shopping

You will not find chain stores and high-street fashion boutiques in Menorca. Shopping on the island means browsing in markets and craft fairs and searching for bargains at small specialist shops.

Where to shop
Maó and Ciutadella are full of individual shops selling everything from candles to chocolate, jewellery to shoes. Prices are not always cheap but service is good and quality is generally high. An open-air clothes and crafts market takes place daily from May to October at the foot of the harbour steps in Maó. Similar markets are held on summer nights in Es Castell and Ciutadella. Towns such as Alaior, Es Mercadal, Fornells and Es Migjorn Gran hold weekly craft markets in summer, and the Saturday morning craft fair at Ferreries runs throughout the year. There are several large shops along the road from Maó to Ciutadella selling souvenirs and local crafts. The Centre Artesanal de Menorca at Es Mercadal is more expensive than the others but features authentic Menorcan arts, crafts and design.

What to buy
Cheese, wine, gin and almond biscuits are popular choices if you want to take home a taste of Menorca. Other good buys are leather shoes or sandals, pottery and jewellery. Look out for 'ecological' T-shirts, made by Ecològica de Menorca, using natural cotton, bright dyes and offbeat designs inspired by the island's history, landscapes and traditions.

ABARCAS

Menorca has a long history of shoemaking, continued today by companies such as Jaime Mascaró and Patricia. One design which is unique to Menorca is the *abarca*, a traditional sandal made by hand-stitching two pieces of leather onto a sole made from recycled car tyres. They have become such a symbol of Menorca that you can even buy miniature ceramic *abarcas* as souvenirs.

Take home a taste of Menorca or treat yourself to a traditional island-made item at a local craft market

Menorca by Night

Menorca does not have the raucous night-life of Mallorca and Ibiza, though there is plenty of late-night action for those who want it. For many people, the best way to spend a summer evening is simply sitting outdoors, enjoying a drink on a harbour-side terrace and watching the sun go down over the sea.

Bars and clubs

The busiest areas for nightlife are Moll de Ponent, facing the ferry station in Maó, and Pla de Sant Joan, behind the harbour in Ciutadella. Both have a number of music clubs and bars which are popular with a young, late-night crowd at weekends. The bigger resorts such as Cala Santa Galdana and Son Bou have discos and nightclubs in summer. Nightlife starts late in Spain, so most of these places do not get going until after midnight and continue until around 6am.

Culture

Look out for posters advertising concerts and theatre performances, or check the listings in *Menorca* daily newspaper or the weekly information sheet available at tourist offices. The Teatre Principal in Maó (▷ 34) has a regular programme of opera, ballet, drama and classical music, with occasional folk and world music events. Other venues include Orfeón Mahonés, a restored 19th-century theatre on Carrer de Gràcia in Maó, and the Teatre Municipal on Plaça des Born in Ciutadella.

MUSIC FESTIVALS

Joventuts Musicals de Ciutadella (www.jjmmciutadella. com) is a classical music festival, with concerts during July and August in the lovely Església dels Socors. A similar festival is organized by Joventuts Musicals de Maó (www. festivaldemusicademao.com) with concerts in the Teatre Principal and Església de Santa Maria. Menorca's International Jazz Festival (www.jazzobert.com) takes place in spring, with visiting artists performing across the island.

Menorca offers a variety of nightlife options, with entertainment to suit all tastes

Eating Out

Eating out is one of the pleasures of a visit to Menorca. The quality of the ingredients is superb, whether you are sharing tapas in a village bar or enjoying fresh seafood beside the sea.

Practicalities
The Spanish eat late—most restaurants in towns and cities open for lunch between 1 and 4 and for dinner from 9pm to midnight. Tapas bars serving sandwiches and snacks stay open all day, and resort restaurants open earlier to cater for Northern European tastes. Only the smartest restaurants may require a reservation and casual dress is acceptable. If you are on a budget, aim to have your main meal at lunchtime, when most restaurants offer a *menú del día*, a set menu with water or wine included at a very reasonable price.

What to eat
Menorcan cuisine is typically Mediterranean, based on fresh island ingredients such as fish, seafood, beef, lamb, vegetables, cheese and olive oil. The Menorcans are proud of their various cured pork sausages, including *sobrasada* and *cuixot*. You may find traditional dishes like *arrós de la terra* (baked wheat with pork and garlic) and *conill amb ametlles* (rabbit with almonds) on offer, but these days many chefs are adapting traditional recipes, combining local ingredients with global influences to create a light, healthy, modern Menorcan cuisine.

MAYONNAISE

According to legend, this popular salad dressing was invented in 1756 during the French occupation of Menorca. The story goes that the Duc de Richelieu and his troops stopped at a farmstead for refreshment. The poor owner, embarrassed that he had no food other than bread to give them, rustled up a sauce from raw eggs and olive oil. The duke liked it so much that he took the recipe back to France and named it *salsa mahonesa* after the town of Mahón.

Enjoy fresh, local food from the land and the sea—often with a beautiful view to accompany your meal

Restaurants by Cuisine

Menorca has restaurants to suit most tastes and budgets. On this page they are listed by cuisine. Some restaurants may be hard to define or may offer more than one style of cooking. For detailed descriptions, see the individual listings in Menorca by Area.

ARGENTINIAN

El Guayacán (▷ 43)

BEACH BAR

Café Susy (▷ 86)

FISH/SEAFOOD

Café Balear (▷ 105)
Can Lluís (▷ 105)
Cap Roig (▷ 43)
Es Cranc (▷ 68)
Cranc Pelut (▷ 68)
Es Pla (▷ 68)
Sa Llagosta (▷ 68)
Varadero (▷ 44)
Vell Parrander (▷ 44)

GRILLED MEAT

El Gallo (▷ 86)
Pa Amb Oli (▷ 106)

ITALIAN

Villa Madrid (▷ 44)

MEDITERRANEAN

El Bósforo (▷ 43)
Ca's Consòl (▷ 105)
El Puchero (▷ 44)

MENORCAN–CREATIVE

Ca N'Olga (▷ 68)
Ca's Ferrer de Sa Font (▷ 105)
Migjorn (▷ 86)
Es Molí de Foc (▷ 43)
Es Tast de Na Silvia (▷ 106)
Pan y Vino (▷ 43)

MENORCAN–TRADITIONAL

58 S'Engolidor (▷ 86)
Binisues (▷ 86)
Ca N'Aguedet (▷ 68)
Sa Quadra (▷ 106)

PIZZA

Casanova (▷ 43)
Oristano (▷ 106)
Il Porto 225 (▷ 44)
Roma (▷ 106)

SPANISH

Ca'n Bep (▷ 105)
Irene (▷ 43)
El Jardí (▷ 105)
Sa Foganya (▷ 44)

SPANISH–GALICIAN

Mesón Galicia (▷ 68)

TAPAS

Bar Peri (▷ 86)
La Cayena (▷ 105)
Sa Lliga (▷ 44)
Sa Mitja Lluna (▷ 68)
Sa Sargantana (▷ 44)
La Tropical (▷ 44)

TRENDY/FUSION

Anakena (▷ 43)
Fusion Café (▷ 105)
Liorna (▷ 86)
Es Puntet (▷ 106)
Ses Forquilles (▷ 44)
Tast (▷ 68)

If You Like...

However you'd like to spend your time in Menorca, these ideas should help you tailor your perfect visit. Each suggestion has a fuller write-up elsewhere in the book.

BIRD'S-EYE VIEWS

Climb the old Roman road to Castell Santa Àgueda (▷ 78) for views over the north coast.
Make the pilgrimage to the chapel on the summit of Monte Toro (▷ 54).
Stand on the cliffs by the lighthouse at Cap de Cavalleria (▷ 49).

LUNCH BESIDE THE SEA

Dine on the beach at Cala Macarella—you don't even have to change out of your swimsuit (▷ 86).
Dip into a bowl of *caldereta de llagosta* beside the harbour in Fornells (▷ 68).
Take your pick of the many waterfront restaurants at Cales Fonts in Es Castell (▷ 43).

Cap de Cavalleria lighthouse (top); Fornells waterfront (above)

KEEPING THE KIDS AMUSED

Put on your swimming costumes and race each other down the waterslides at Aquacenter in Cala En Blanes (▷ 103).
See Menorcan red cows and other rare breeds of farm animals at Lloc de Menorca (▷ 64).
Take them to a show at Son Martorellet to see Menorcan horses prancing and dancing in fiesta mood (▷ 84).

Making a splash (above)

MYSTERIOUS ANCIENT MONUMENTS

Take a look inside a prehistoric burial chamber at Naveta des Tudons (▷ 92).
Unravel the mystery of the *taulas* at Trepucó (▷ 38) and Talatí de Dalt (▷ 38).
Walk around the walls of Son Catlar, a megalithic village blending into the modern countryside (▷ 96).

Explore Menorca's megalithic past (above)

PARTYING TILL DAWN

Chill out at Cova d'en Xoroi, Menorca's most unusual nightclub, in a cave up on the cliffs (▷ 67).

Dance the night away at Salsa, the best place to hear Cuban music, beside the harbour at Maó (▷ 42).

Look out for live bands at Jazzbah, one of several late-night clubs behind the harbour in Ciutadella (▷ 103).

SAMPLING LOCAL CUISINE

Be prepared to be surprised by the new-wave Menorcan cuisine at Migjorn (▷ 86) or Tast (▷ 68).

Taste traditional island dishes like crab with snails or rabbit with figs at Ca N'Aguedet (▷ 68).

Tuck into steak with Mahón cheese at El Gallo, a farmhouse restaurant specializing in grilled meat (▷ 86).

Live music (top); Menorcan cuisine is varied and tasty (above)

REMOTE BEACHES AND BAYS

Follow the coast path from Binimel-là to the beach at Cala Pregonda (▷ 81).

Leave your car behind and walk through the woods to Cala del Pilar (▷ 73).

Take a boat trip to Cala Trebalúger from Cala En Bosc (▷ 99) or Cala Santa Galdana (▷ 76) in summer.

Take a boat trip (above); visit Ferreries for the market (below)

SHOPPING FOR SOUVENIRS

Catch one of the craft fairs which take place in summer, or the Saturday morning craft market at Ferreries (▷ 81).

Treat yourself to a pair of hand-made leather sandals at S'Abarca (▷ 40) or Ca'n Doblas (▷ 84).

Visit the farm shop at Hort de Sant Patrici to stock up on cheese, sausages and local wine (▷ 79).

SLEEPING IN STYLE

Escape the summer heat at Hotel Sant Ignasi (▷ 112), a rural hotel with shady gardens and a pool.

Get away from it all at Biniarroca (▷ 112), an artistic and romantic rural retreat.

Sleep in a Georgian townhouse at Casa Albertí in Maó (▷ 110), an elegant bolthole in the heart of the city.

SOMETHING FOR NOTHING

Go to the trotting races in Maó and Ciutadella at weekends—free unless you decide to have a bet (▷ 42, 103).

Help yourself to free samples of gin and liqueurs at Destilerías Xoriguer (▷ 36).

Visit monuments on Sundays, when sights such as Fort Marlborough (▷ 28) and Naveta des Tudons (▷ 92) have free admission.

A quiet retreat in Maó (top) or the excitement of the trotting races (above)

EXPLORING MILITARY HISTORY

Learn about the 18th-century battles for Menorca at the Military Museum in Es Castell (▷ 24).

Stare down the gun barrel of an enormous cannon and walk through the loophole gallery at Fortalesa de la Mola (▷ 26).

Explore the underground tunnels of Fort Sant Felip (▷ 37), an abandoned fortress at the entrance to Maó harbour.

The remains of Fort Sant Felip (above); take the time to enjoy the view (below)

ROMANTIC VIEWS

Climb the hill from Cala Santa Galdana (▷ 76) to Mirador de Sa Punta for sweeping views over the south coast.

Sit on the steps by Castell de Sant Nicolau in Ciutadella (▷ 97), gazing at the mountains of Mallorca across the sea.

Watch the sun set behind the lighthouse on the cliffs at Cap d'Artrutx (▷ 101).

Menc...by Area

Maó (Mahón) stands on a cliff, protected by one of the world's great natural harbours. It may be the Menorcan capital but it has the relaxed feel of a small provincial town. With its forts, towers and remnants of British rule, the harbour bears witness to Menorca's long and varied history.

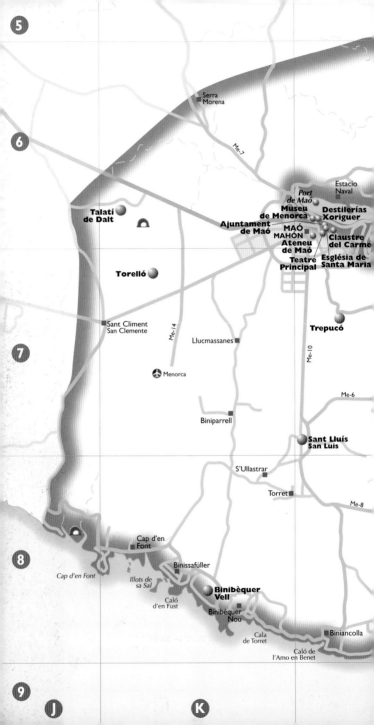

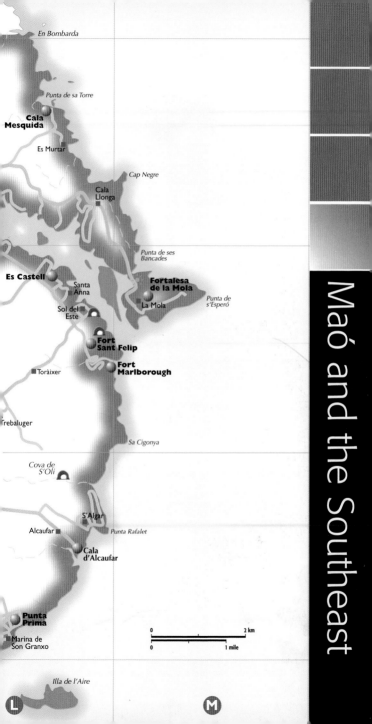

En Bombarda

Punta de sa Torre

Cala Mesquida

Es Murtar

Cap Negre

Cala Llonga

Punta de ses Bancades

Es Castell

Santa Anna

Fortalesa de la Mola

La Mola

Punta de s'Esperó

Sol del Este

Fort Sant Felip

Toràixer

Fort Marlborough

Trebaluger

Sa Cigonya

Cova de S'Oli

S'Algar

Alcaufar

Punta Rafalet

Cala d'Alcaufar

Punta Prima

Marina de Son Granxo

Illa de l'Aire

Es Castell

If you want to trace the British heritage in Menorca, there is no better place than Es Castell. This solid garrison town retains a dignified, colonial presence and is still preferred by British residents today.

A change of name Built by the British during their second occupation of the island to house troops from Fort Sant Felip (▷ 37), the town was originally named Georgetown after King George III. When the Spanish took control of Menorca, they renamed it Villacarlos after Carlos III and it is now known simply as Es Castell (the castle).

British base With streets laid out in a neat grid plan around a central parade ground, Es Castell has the feel of a military town. The parade ground is now the main square, Plaça de S'Esplanada.

Clockwise from top left: the former military parade ground, now the main square, Plaça de S'Esplanada; the attractive harbour at Cales Fonts; the Georgian town hall on Plaça de S'Esplanada

On one side is the town hall, topped by a British clock tower; on the other, the old Cala Corb barracks house the Museu Militar (Military Museum). The museum contains artillery, maps, portraits and scale models depicting the island's history, particularly the 18th-century period of British occupation. The creek at Cala Corb, from which the barracks took their name, is called 'Corpse Cove', because of the bodies that would wash up there from the military hospital in Maó harbour.

First light As the easternmost town in Spain, Es Castell is the first place to catch the rising sun each morning. A short walk from Plaça de S'Esplanada leads down to the picturesque harbour at Cales Fonts, which is buzzing on summer evenings with restaurants and bars in the old boathouses beneath the cliffs.

THE BASICS

➕ L7
🚌 2 from Maó

Museu Militar
www.museomilitarmenorca.com
✉ Plaça de S'Esplanada 19
☎ 971 362100
🕐 Jun–end Aug Mon–Fri and first Sun of the month 10–1; Sep–end May Mon, Wed, Fri and first Sun of the month 10–1
♿ Few
💷 Moderate

Fortalesa de la Mola

HIGHLIGHTS

- View over Cala d'es Clot
- View from Hornworks
- Loophole gallery walk
- Vickers cannon

TIPS

- Take a picnic and spend all day here in summer—there are wonderful walks and views from the cliffs but you must stick to the marked paths at all times.
- In summer, you can take a boat to La Mola from the harbourside at Maó.

The climax of a visit to the fort on La Mola is staring down the gun barrel of an enormous cannon—a powerful reminder of the strategic importance of Maó harbour and its place in Menorcan history.

Royal fort The construction of the enormous fortress of Isabel II, named in honour of the Spanish queen, was begun in 1848. It was built at the entrance to Maó harbour on the rocky promontory of La Mola to defend Menorca from attack by land and sea. During the Spanish Civil War, Republican forces rounded up military officers and shot them here—a plaque pays tribute to those who died 'for God and Spain' in 1936. Later, it was used as a political prison for opponents of General Franco's regime. The army finally left the site in 1999.

Clockwise from left: the interior of the Fortalesa de la Mola demonstrates the strength of the building; the main gate to the fort; panoramic view of the fort complex on the headland of La Mola; exhibitions are held in a gallery space within the fort

Visiting La Mola You can explore the fort on your own with the help of an audioguide, or join one of the fascinating guided tours. The full circuit is 5km (3 miles) and takes about two hours on foot, though there are regular minibus transfers between the main sights. One highlight is the loophole gallery, a series of casemates almost 400m (438 yards) in length, with loopholes to enable the inhabitants of the fort to defend the moat. Visiting the loophole gallery involves a long underground walk and a climb of 50 steps—if you want to avoid this there is an alternative route above ground. The tour ends with a visit to the engine room of a Vickers coastal cannon, high on the cliffs pointing out to sea with a range of 35km (22 miles). This is the largest gun ever to be built in Spain—but it was never fired in anger as the fort never came under attack.

THE BASICS

www.fortalesalamola.com

➕ M7

✉ La Mola

☎ 971 364040

🕐 Jun–end Sep daily 10–8; May and Oct daily 10–6; Nov–end Apr Tue–Sun 10–2

🍽 Café in summer (€)

♿ Good; call in advance

💰 Expensive

🚢 From Maó in summer

❓ Guided tours of the fort daily 10.30, 12.30, 5.30 (also Wed 11); tours of the Vickers battery daily 1 and 5

Fort Marlborough

TOP 25

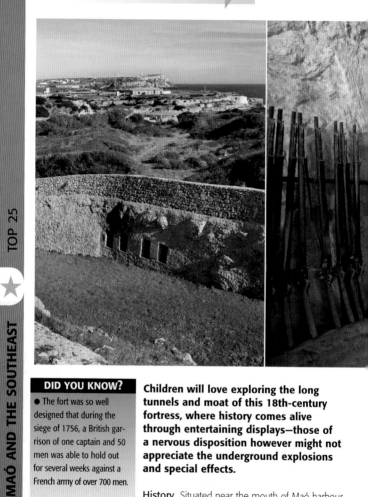

DID YOU KNOW?

● The fort was so well designed that during the siege of 1756, a British garrison of one captain and 50 men was able to hold out for several weeks against a French army of over 700 men.

TIP

● There is limited parking at the fort itself, so leave your car in the large parking area on the road from Es Castell and follow the marked path down to Cala de Sant Esteve.

Children will love exploring the long tunnels and moat of this 18th-century fortress, where history comes alive through entertaining displays—those of a nervous disposition however might not appreciate the underground explosions and special effects.

History Situated near the mouth of Maó harbour in the narrow creek of Cala de Sant Esteve, Fort Marlborough was built by the British between 1710 and 1726 and named after Sir John Churchill, Duke of Marlborough, the most distinguished soldier of his generation. Together with nearby Fort Sant Felip (▷ 37), it formed part of the defence system of Maó harbour—though stories of underwater tunnels linking the two forts have been discounted. The fort was successfully

Far-reaching views from Fort Marlborough (left); informative displays bring a visit to Fort Marlborough to life (right)

besieged by the French during their invasion of 1756 and again in 1781 by the Spanish fleet. The present seven-sided fortress dates from 1798, when the British also added the Martello defence tower, Torre d'en Penjat, which overlooks Fort Marlborough from the hilltop.

The visit A visit to the fort begins with an audio-visual show, which provides an introduction to Menorca's 18th-century history. Then, the long entrance tunnel leads to the counterscarp gallery, ingeniously hewn out of the rock. As you follow the gallery around the edge of the moat, look out for hidden explosions coming from the counter-mine passages to your right. Eventually, you climb to the rooftop for views across Maó harbour with the ruins of Fort Sant Felip in the foreground and Fortalesa de la Mola (▷ 26) in the distance.

THE BASICS

✚ M7
✉ Cala de Sant Esteve
☎ 902 929015
🕐 Early Apr–end Sep Tue–Sat 9.30–8.30, Sun–Mon 9.30–3; Easter–early Apr and Oct–Dec Tue–Sun 9.30–3; closed Jan–Easter
🍴 None
♿ Few
💰 Moderate; free on Sun

Maó: Museu de Menorca

HIGHLIGHTS

● The cloister
● Skeleton of *Myotragus Balearicus*
● Bronze figure of Imhotep, an Egyptian god
● Roman mosaic
● Scrap metal from a Roman shipwreck off Cap de Favàritx

TIP

● The octagonal chapel in the Church of Sant Francesc next door is an example of the ornate Churrigueresque (Spanish baroque) style.

For an understanding of Menorcan history, visit the Museum of Menorca, whose exhibits span almost 5,000 years. It is worth the entrance fee just to see the cloister, where concerts are held on summer evenings.

The lower floor The museum is laid out over two storeys around the cloister of the Convent de Sant Francesc, a Franciscan monastery dissolved in 1835 and later used as a library and naval college. The first-floor displays focus on ancient history, with burial hoards from sites such as Cales Coves (▷ 48) and Naveta des Tudons (▷ 92) and a bronze figure of a young bull discovered at Torralba d'en Salord (▷ 59). Also here is a complete skeleton of *Myotragus Balearicus*, a goat-like mammal which once thrived on Menorca

The tranquil cloister of the former Franciscan monastery in Maó which now houses the Museu de Menorca (left); details of the Church of Sant Francesc, which adjoins the museum (right, top and bottom)

but became extinct after the arrival of the first humans. A separate room is devoted to the Roman occupation of Menorca. The display here includes a mosaic from a 6th-century basilica that stood on an island in Maó harbour.

The upper floor The second-floor galleries begin with the Islamic conquest of Menorca in AD903 and continue through to the 20th century. Of particular interest are the maps and paintings of 18th-century Menorca, including the period of British rule. There is an enjoyable collection of wooden figurines, created by the Monjo brothers in the late 19th century to caricature local celebrities. Apart from the cloister, the only vestiges of the old monastery are the brightly decorated ceramic panels depicting the Stations of the Cross and religious motifs.

THE BASICS

➕ a2
✉ Pla des Monestir, Maó
☎ 971 350955
🕐 Apr–end Oct Tue–Fri 9.30–2, 6–8, Sat 10–2, 6–8, Sun 10–2; Nov–end Mar Tue–Sat 9.30–2, Sun 10–2
🍴 None
♿ Good
💲 Inexpensive

A relaxed cruise around Maó harbour is an enjoyable experience in itself, but it is also a voyage back to the 18th century, when great powers fought over Menorca and the harbour at Maó was the prize.

Strategic base When Britain and France were struggling for control of the western Mediterranean, Menorca was a key battleground. The reason was the harbour at Maó, 5km (3 miles) long and the world's second longest natural harbour. Located at the crossroads of naval and trade routes, both sides wanted the harbour so they would have a secure winter base for their ships. The British needed a naval base between Malta and Gibraltar, while the French wanted to control the route between their ports at Toulon and Algiers.

The impressive natural harbour at Maó was once prized for its strategic position in the Mediterranean. Today it is a stop-off for cruises and pleasure craft

On the water You can explore the harbour on a one-hour boat trip, which departs from the quayside at the foot of the harbour steps in Maó. Several companies offer cruises, including Yellow Catamarans, whose triple-deck boats have a sun deck, main deck and underwater viewing area. You will see the 18th-century British naval station and English cemetery, and pass Illa del Rei (King's Island), where Alfons III landed when he captured Menorca in 1287. The British later built a military hospital here and renamed it Bloody Island. Near the mouth of the harbour, Illa del Llatzeret is a former quarantine island, separated from the mainland by an artificial canal. Keep an eye out for the striking pink colonial mansion overlooking the harbour on its eastern shore. Known as Golden Farm, the British admiral Lord Nelson is said, without much evidence, to have stayed here in 1799.

THE BASICS

www.yellowcatamarans.com

✚ c1

✉ Moll de Llevant 12, Maó

☎ 639 676351

⏰ Departures May–end Oct Mon–Sat every 45 minutes from 10.30–4.30, Sun 10.45, 12.15, 1.45; Apr up to four sailings daily (times vary, phone for details); Nov–end Mar group bookings only

🍴 Bar (€)

♿ Few; access to main deck only

💲 Expensive

Maó: Teatre Principal

TOP
25

Enjoy a performance in the comfort of the sumptuously restored Teatre Principal

THE BASICS

www.teatremao.org
⊞ b3
✉ Costa d'en Deià 40, Maó
☎ 971 355776
🕐 Box office Tue–Sat 11.30–1.30; also Thu–Fri 6.30–8.30 and one hour before performances
♿ Good
👐 Varies

DID YOU KNOW?

● The Menorcan baritone Joan Pons played Falstaff at the opening night of the restored theatre in 2001.
● The railings in the lower tier of boxes were designed to shield women's legs from public view.

The Teatre Principal, an elegant 19th-century opera house, has been restored to its former glory and is once again the focus of Maó's cultural life.

History There are records of plays being staged on this site since the 18th century—the Museum of Decorative Arts in Paris has paintings depicting a drama by Molière performed at the Mahón Comedy Theatre during the French occupation. The present building dates from 1829, when Italian impresario Giovanni Palaggi commissioned what is now the oldest opera house in Spain. The neoclassical façade, built from local stone, was added in 1859. The theatre was restored during the late 20th century and reopened in 2001.

The theatre today A bronze sculpture of Thalia, the Greek muse of comedy, by Menorcan artist Maties Quetglas, stands outside the theatre, holding a comic mask in her hand. The modern foyer leads to the auditorium, built in the shape of a horseshoe with over 800 seats and three tiers of boxes. The plush red stage curtain depicts three female figures representing comedy, tragedy and dance, surmounted by the coat of arms of Maó and portraits of opera singers and composers.

What's on? There are no regular tours of the theatre, so the only way to see inside is to buy a ticket for a show. Performances of drama, ballet and classical music take place throughout the year, with occasional pop and folk music concerts and a spring opera season.

More to See

Maó

AJUNTAMENT DE MAÓ
www.ajmao.org

Maó's town hall dates from 1613 but the present building was completed in 1789. A stone staircase leads to the portico, which is topped by a baroque tower housing an English clock and the city's coat of arms. During office hours, you are welcome to look around. The council chamber contains the Gallery of Illustrious Menorcans, a series of portraits of distinguished figures from the island beginning with Dr Mateu Orfila (1787–1853), court physician to French king Louis XVIII and the founder of modern toxicology.

➕ b2 ✉ Plaça Constitució 1, Maó ☎ 971 369800 🕐 Mon–Sat 8–2 ♿ None 💶 Free

ATENEU DE MAÓ
www.ateneumao.org

This scientific, literary and artistic association was founded in 1905 and continues to play a central role in Maó's intellectual and cultural life. The small museum includes exhibitions of geology, natural history, maps and paintings by local artist Joan Vives Llull (1901–82). Don't miss the collection of 18th-century Catalan pottery, with decorative tiles depicting musicians, farmers and scenes of everyday life.

➕ a3 ✉ Sa Rovellada de Dalt 25, Maó ☎ 971 360553 🕐 Sep–end May Mon–Fri 10–2, 4–10, Sat 10–2, 5–9; Jun Mon–Fri 10–2, 5.30–10, Sat 10–2; Jul–end Aug Mon–Sat 10–2 ♿ Good 💶 Free

CLAUSTRE DEL CARME

The cloisters of a former Carmelite convent have been used as a school, law court and prison but today they house Maó's atmospheric market. Folk dance displays take place in the cloister on summer evenings. Just off the cloister, the Museu Hernández Sanz Hernández Mora features furniture, maps, books and paintings collected by a local historian.

➕ c2 ✉ Plaça del Carme, Maó
Museu Hernández Sanz Hernández Mora
✉ Claustre del Carme ☎ 971 350597 🕐 May–end Oct daily 10–1; Nov–end Apr Mon–Sat 10–1 ♿ Few 💶 Free

The main entrance of the Ajuntament de Maó

The bustling market in the Claustre del Carme

DESTILERÍAS XORIGUER
www.xoriguer.es

Gin was introduced to Menorca by British sailors in the 18th century, and it is still produced at this distillery on the waterfront in Maó. The factory shop offers free tastings of gin and various gin-based liqueurs flavoured with coffee, peppermint, chamomile, rosehip and herbs, but there are no factory tours and little insight into the production process.

🔂 b2 ✉ Moll de Ponent 91, Maó ☎ 971 362197 🕐 May–end Oct Mon–Fri 8–6, Sat 10–2; Nov–end Apr Mon–Fri 9–1, 4–6 ♿ None 🖐 Free

ESGLÉSIA DE SANTA MARIA

This huge 18th-century church is the nearest thing Maó has to a cathedral. During the summer months, there are daily music recitals on the Swiss-built organ, installed in 1810. Behind the church, Plaça de la Conquesta is dominated by a statue of Alfons III of Aragón, conqueror of Menorca in 1287.

🔂 c2 ✉ Plaça Constitució, Maó ☎ 971 363949 🕐 Daily 8–12, 6–8.30 ♿ Good; entrance on Plaça de la Conquesta 🖐 Free ❓ Organ recitals May–Oct Mon–Sat 11am

The Southeast
BINIBÈQUER VELL

This so-called 'fishermen's village' was designed in 1972 as a reaction against the high-rise tourist developments elsewhere on the coast—but with its whitewashed holiday apartments, narrow lanes and Moorish-Mediterranean architecture, it has become a pastiche of 'the other Menorca' and a dubious tourist attraction in itself. On summer weekends, the people of Maó head to nearby Binibèquer beach and its famous beach bar, Los Bucaneros.

🔂 K8 🚌 93 from Maó in summer

CALA D'ALCAUFAR

The narrow inlet at Cala d'Alcaufar was the site of the first British landing on Menorca in 1708. These days, it is a pleasant, low-key beach resort, with whitewashed cottages and boathouses reaching down to the water's edge. A path behind the beach leads

The lantern tower of the Església de Santa Maria in Maó

Dine al fresco in Binibèquer Vell

onto the cliffs and crosses the headland to an 18th-century watchtower before continuing along the coast to Punta Prima (▷ below right).

🚩 L8 🚌 91 from Maó in summer

CALA MESQUIDA

This small seaside village on the far side of Maó harbour is where many Menorcans have their summer houses. The sandy beach shelters between two rocky headlands, one of which is crowned by a British-built Martello tower. Locals come here to eat fresh fish at Cap Roig (▷ 43), one of the finest fish restaurants on the island.

🚩 L6 🍴 Cap Roig (€€)

FORT SANT FELIP

This once powerful fortress at the entrance to Maó harbour now stands abandoned, neglected and covered with weeds. Destroyed by Spanish troops when they captured Menorca from the British in 1782, it is almost invisible above ground—but underground the fortress survives largely intact, with its well, powder magazines and 10km (6 miles) of tunnels where up to 4,000 British soldiers lived and died under siege. The fort still belongs to the army and can only be visited on a guided tour, which lasts about 90 minutes and includes lots of underground passages and steep steps. There are night-time tours in summer, with visitors walking through the tunnels by torchlight.

🚩 L7 ✉ Fort Sant Felip, Es Castell ☎ 971 362100 🕐 Jun Thu 5pm, Sun 10am; Jul–end Sep Thu, Sun 10am; Mar–end May and Oct–end Nov Sat 10am; closed Dec–end Feb. Night tours mid–Jun to mid–Sep Sun 8.30–11.30; these must be pre-booked ♿ None 💷 Moderate

PUNTA PRIMA

This sprawling resort at the southeastern tip of Menorca has one of the island's longest beaches. There are views across the water to Illa de l'Aire, an uninhabited island with a lighthouse. From the north end of the beach, a restored section of the Camí de Cavalls coast path leads to Cala d'Alcaufar (▷ 36).

🚩 L8 🚌 92 from Maó in summer

The remains of Fort Sant Felip are washed by waves, while the headland of La Mola rises behind

The sheltered sandy beach at Cala Mesquida

SANT LLUÍS

Founded by the French in 1761 and named after King Louis IX, this is one of Menorca's most attractive inland towns. The restored windmill on the main street, Molí de Dalt, contains a small museum of agricultural tools.

🔲 L7 🚌 3 from Maó

Molí de Dalt ✉ Carrer Sant Lluís 4
☎ 971 151084 🕐 Jun–end Sep Mon–Fri 10–2, 5–8, Sat 10–1, Sun 11–1; Oct–end May Mon–Fri 10–2, Sat 10–1 ♿ Good
✋ Inexpensive; free on Sun

TALATÍ DE DALT

This romantic ancient monument stands undisturbed in the middle of farmland, surrounded by meadows, sheep shelters and stone walls. In the middle is a *taula* sanctuary, with one small *taula* leaning against another, a horseshoe of stones sheltered by a wild olive tree and an immense *talaiot* standing guard nearby.

🔲 K6 ✉ Signposted off Maó to Ciutadella road, km4 🕐 May–end Sep daily 10am–sunset; free access in winter ♿ None
✋ Moderate; free Oct–end Apr

TORELLÓ

The 6th-century Byzantine Church of Es Fornàs de Torelló was discovered in 1956 by a farmer ploughing his fields. The basilica now has a protective roof, and you can access the viewing platform to admire the mosaics of peacocks, palm trees and lions.

🔲 K7 ✉ Camí de Torelló (signposted off Maó to Sant Climent road) 🕐 Free access
♿ Few ✋ Free

TREPUCÓ

The settlement of the prehistoric village at Trepucó probably reached its peak at the height of the Talaiotic culture in Menorca around 1300BC. A large *talaiot* stands at its heart with a smaller one nearby. Both the *talaiot* and the *taula* enclosure are surrounded by a star-shaped defensive wall, built by the French in 1782.

🔲 L7 ✉ Camí de Trepucó (signposted off Maó to Sant Lluís road) 🕐 Easter–early Apr and Oct Tue–Sun 9–3; early–Apr–end Sep Tue–Sat 9–9, Sun 9–3; Nov–Easter free access ♿ None ✋ Inexpensive; free on Sun and Nov–Easter

Sant Lluís' restored windmill houses a small museum of agricultural tools

The remains at Talatí de Dalt

A Walk around Maó

With old-fashioned shopping streets and café-lined squares, Maó is a city for strolling. This easy walk takes in most of the main sights.

DISTANCE: 2.5km (1.5 miles)   **ALLOW:** 1 hour (approximately)

START

BUS STATION
a3

1 Walk downhill from the bus station to reach Plaça de S'Esplanada. Keep right across the square and continue downhill along Carrer de Ses Moreres.

2 Keep straight ahead as the road becomes pedestrian-only, now named Costa de Sa Plaça, and drops steeply towards the port. Pass Plaça de Colon, a pretty square of palm trees and open-air cafés, then turn right along Carrer Nou.

3 Follow this busy shopping street to Plaça Reial, then turn left along S'Arravaleta, emerging opposite Claustre del Carme. Turn left and walk downhill to Plaça d'Espanya, passing the fish market, dating from 1927, on your right.

4 Ignore the steps leading down to the harbour and continue around the white railings to Plaça de la Conquesta, passing Casa Mir, the finest example of Modernista (art nouveau) architecture in Maó.

END

BUS STATION

7 Cross Plaça Bastió and follow Carrer Bastió to its end. Turn right along Carrer de Ses Moreres to return to the bus station via Plaça de S'Esplanada.

6 Leaving the museum, take the right fork along Carrer de Sant Jeroni. The road bends right to become Carrer des Rector Mort, arriving beside Pont de Sant Roc, the only surviving part of Maó's 14th-century walls.

5 Head diagonally across Plaça de la Conquesta and take Carrer d'Alfons III to arrive at the town hall. Turn right and follow the road round to your left to reach Carrer d'Isabel II, with its handsome 18th-century Georgian houses. The road ends at the Museu de Menorca (▷ 30).

WALK

Shopping

BODEGUES BINIFADET
www.binifadet.com
This winery on the outskirts of Sant Lluís offers tours of the natural limestone cellars and tastings of Chardonnay, Merlot, Syrah and Muscat wines.
🔢 L7 ✉ Ses Barraques, Sant Lluís ☎ 971 150715

ES BOUER DE BINIBECA
Farmhouse shop selling Mahón cheese and other local products, just outside Binibèquer Vell on the road to Sant Lluís.
🔢 K8 ✉ Carretera Binibèquer-Sant Lluís ☎ 971 156572

LA CERERIA
This arty candle shop in an old Georgian townhouse sells a wide range of candles and candle holders, plus stylish accessories and pretty, feminine dresses.
🔢 b2 ✉ Carrer d'Isabel II 6, Maó ☎ 971 352540

CLAUSTRE DEL CARME
Maó's indoor market hall, in the charming setting of the old cloisters (▷ 35), has stalls selling fresh fruit and vegetables as well as island wines and cheeses. The shops around the outside sell Menorcan sandals and other gifts, and there is a supermarket in the basement.
🔢 c2 ✉ Plaça del Carme, Maó

DESTILEREÍAS XORIGUER
www.xoriguer.es
The factory shop on the waterfront at Maó sells gin and liqueurs from the Xoriguer distillery. A winter favourite is *calent*, a sweet, spicy liqueur with aniseed and cinnamon, usually served warm. You can taste before you buy.
🔢 b2 ✉ Moll de Ponent 91, Maó ☎ 971 362197

DIVERTIMENTO
Spanish, Menorcan and international CDs including jazz, folk and classical music.
🔢 b3 ✉ Plaça de Colon 9, Maó ☎ 971 352844

FRANCISCO LORA
Hand-made pottery by Paco Lora Buzón is on display at this boutique. Nearby, shops along the waterfront sell clothing, sandals and crafts, and there is an outdoor

MENORCAN WINE
After decades of inactivity, the Menorcan wine industry has made great strides since the awarding of the 'Vi de la Terra Illa de Menorca' denomination in 2002. Some of the best wines are Malvasia from Sa Cudia and Merlot from Binifadet (▷ above), who also make Menorca's first sparkling wine. Other labels to look out for are Ferrer de Muntpalau and Rubí del Mediterraneo.

market at the foot of the harbour steps in summer.
🔢 c2 ✉ Moll de Ponent 33–36, Maó ☎ 971 350303

JAIME MASCARÓ
www.jaimemascaro.com
Stylish men's and women's shoes by Jaime and Ursula Mascaró, seen on the catwalks of Europe.
🔢 b3 ✉ Carrer de Ses Moreres 29, Maó ☎ 971 360568

LLIBRERIA FUNDACIÓ
Bookshop with a good selection of books on Menorca, including foreign language editions.
🔢 b3 ✉ Costa de Sa Plaça 14, Maó ☎ 971 363543

S'ABARCA
The best place to buy a pair of Menorcan *abarcas* (sandals), which are handmade on site.
🔢 d2 (fold-out map) ✉ Moll de Llevant 21, Maó ☎ 971 353462

SIBARITAS
Delicatessen on the outskirts of Maó selling cheese, wine, olive oil, cured meats, chocolate and other treats.
🔢 f5 (fold-out map) ✉ Camí d'es Castell 271, Maó ☎ 971 357629

EL TURRONERO
This famous old pastry shop, founded in 1894, sells home-made nougat plus ice-cream and fresh lemonade in summer.
🔢 b3 ✉ Carrer Nou 22, Maó ☎ 971 362898

Entertainment and Activities

AKELARRE

www.akelarrejazz.es
This jazz and blues club is a popular late-night spot, with live music most weekends. It is the start of a busy nightlife strip with bars and discos built into the cliff face at the foot of Costa des General.

➕ b2 ✉ Moll de Ponent 41–43, Maó ☎ 971 368520 ◷ Summer daily 3pm–4am; winter Mon–Thu 7pm–3am, Fri–Sun 3pm–4am

CASINO MARÍTIM

www.casinomaritimo.es
Menorca's only casino is high on a cliff: an elevator takes you up from the harbourside entrance at Cala Figuera. Games include poker, blackjack and American roulette, plus slot machines. Bring your passport as you must be over 18 to enter. Smart dress is expected.

➕ f2 (fold-out map) ✉ Moll de Llevant 287, Maó ☎ 971 364962 ◷ Daily 8pm–5am

CASINO SANT CLIMENT

www.casinosantcliment.com
Just outside Maó in the village of Sant Climent, this restaurant hosts weekly jazz sessions in the summer months.

➕ K7 ✉ Carrer Sant Jaume 4, Sant Climent ☎ 971 153418 ◷ Jazz nights May– end Oct Tue 9.30pm–1am

ES CAU

Set inside a fishermen's cave in the harbour of Cala Corb, Es Cau is the best place to hear traditional Spanish and Menorcan folk songs. Singer Biel and guitarist Paco have been entertaining their friends here for over 40 years, and anyone is welcome to join in.

➕ L7 ✉ Cala Corb, Es Castell ◷ Daily 10pm–1am

HIPODROM DE MAÓ

www.hipodromdemao.com
Trotting races—a form of horse-racing in which the jockey sits in a small cart behind the horse— are held every weekend at this hippodrome on the road from Maó to Sant Lluís.

➕ Off map at a5 ✉ Avinguda Josep Anselm Clavé 400, Maó ☎ 971 368662 ◷ May–end Oct Sat 6pm; Nov–end Apr Sun 11am

---

VIVEMENORCA!

Maó's basketball team, ViveMenorca (previously La Salle Mahón; www.menorca-basquet.com) was promoted to the Spanish premier league in 2005. Matches against top Spanish clubs such as Real Madrid take place between October and May at the Pavelló Menorca, a purpose-built stadium on the outskirts of Maó. Tickets can be bought at the stadium in advance (Mon–Fri 9–2, 5–8) or 90 minutes before the match. Check local newspapers for details of upcoming fixtures.

MENORCA CRICKET CLUB

www.menorcacricketclub.com
England's national sport is kept alive by a small group of expats in Sant Lluís. Visitors are welcome to watch matches, or take part in the open games in summer.

➕ K7 ✉ Biniparrell, Sant Lluís ☎ 971 350808 ◷ Fixtures Apr–Oct; open games Jul and Aug Wed 10.30 and Sat 1.30

ORFEÓN MAHONÉS

This choral society was founded in 1890. The original theatre, restored in 2007, now hosts performances of drama and classical music.

➕ b4 ✉ Carrer Verge de Gràcia 155, Maó ☎ 971 363942

SALSA

Lively late-night bar with Cuban music and dancing, popular with local Latin Americans and crews from visiting ships.

➕ c2 ✉ Moll de Ponent 29, Maó ☎ 971 352996 ◷ Summer daily 10pm–4am; winter Fri–Sat 10pm–4am

TEATRE PRINCIPAL

www.teatremao.com
This elegant opera house (▷ 34) hosts a year-round programme of theatre, music and dance.

➕ b3 ✉ Costa d'en Deià 40, Maó ☎ 971 355776 ◷ Box office Tue–Sat 11.30– 1.30; also Thu–Fri 6.30–8.30 and one hour before performances

Restaurants

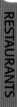

PRICES

Prices are approximate, based on a 3-course meal for one person.
€€€	over €40
€€	€20–€40
€	under €20

ANAKENA (€€€)

www.anakenarestoran.com
With sofas and wicker chairs in the gardens of an elegant country house, and a Japanese-inspired menu, a meal at Anakena is an experience. Expect small portions of light, healthy food, which is fresh and tasty.
🔟 L7 ⊠ S'Uestrà 90, Sant Lluís ☎ 971 156727 🕐 Dinner; closed Oct–May

EL BÓSFORO (€€)

Enjoy Mediterranean meat and fish dishes here while overlooking the harbour. At lunchtime, the bar serves a good-value set menu with a hint of Middle Eastern influence.
🔟 d2 (fold-out map) ⊠ Moll de Llevant 60, Maó ☎ 971 369496 🕐 Lunch and dinner; closed Sun and Nov

CAP ROIG (€€€)

Dramatically situated on a clifftop high above the sea, this restaurant offers some of the finest views and freshest fish in Menorca. The name of the restaurant means 'scorpion fish', which features on the menu alongside sardines, prawns, lobster and rice dishes. If you want to be sure of a table, book ahead. Get there by following the narrow track to the right as you enter Cala Mesquida from Maó.
🔟 L6 ⊠ Cala Mesquida ☎ 971 188383 🕐 Lunch and dinner; closed Mon

CASANOVA (€€)

A lively pizzeria near the foot of the harbour steps in Maó serving home-made pasta and authentic wood-fired Italian pizzas. Choose from unusual offerings like apple and gorgonzola pizza, or rocket and Spanish ham.
🔟 c2 ⊠ Moll de Ponent 15, Maó ☎ 971 354169 🕐 Lunch and dinner; closed Mon

EL GUAYACÁN (€€)

This Argentinian restaurant on the promenade serves tapas, fresh fish and a *menu criollo* which includes a generous portion of grilled meat with spicy *chimichurri* sauce.

OPENING TIMES

Although the opening times listed on these pages act as a guide, many restaurants stay open all hours in summer but only open at weekends or close down altogether between October and May. It is rarely necessary to book, but if you want to be sure a restaurant is open, it is best to telephone in advance.

🔟 d2 (fold-out map) ⊠ Moll de Llevant 139, Maó ☎ 971 360528 🕐 Daily lunch and dinner

IRENE (€€)

With a terrace overlooking the harbour at Cales Fonts, Irene serves modern interpretations of Spanish and Menorcan cuisine. A blackboard lists the fresh fish of the day.
🔟 L7 ⊠ Carrer Sa Font 1, Es Castell ☎ 971 354788 🕐 Daily lunch and dinner

ES MOLÍ DE FOC (€€)

www.molidefoc.com
Valencian chef Vicent Vila creates sophisticated Spanish cuisine in an old flour mill in Sant Climent. Specialties include black paella, duck breast with strawberry sauce, and Mahón cheese and fig ice-cream. With modern art on the walls and a candlelit courtyard in summer, this is a good place for a romantic meal.
🔟 K7 ⊠ Carrer Sant Llorenç 65, Sant Climent ☎ 971 153222 🕐 Tue–Sat lunch and dinner, Sun lunch (also Jul–end Aug Mon lunch and dinner); closed mid-Dec to Jan

PAN Y VINO (€€€)

French chef Patrick James uses local seasonal produce to create delicious meat and fish dishes at this old farmhouse in Torret. The name means 'bread and wine'.
🔟 K8 ⊠ Camí de la Coixa 3, Torret, Sant Lluís

☎ 971 150201 🕒 Summer Wed–Mon dinner; winter Sun lunch, Fri–Sat dinner

IL PORTO 225 (€€)

www.ilporto225.com
This open-plan restaurant on the harbourside specializes in pizza, but also serves a variety of pasta dishes, salads, grilled meat and fish.
➕ e2 (fold-out map)
✉ Moll de Llevant 225, Maó
☎ 971 354426 🕒 Lunch and dinner; closed Wed

EL PUCHERO (€€)

This beautiful, traditional Menorcan house, dating from 1880, has been converted into a cosy restaurant. The menu spans Europe.
➕ L7 ✉ Calle Gran 67, Es Castell ☎ 971 356983
🕒 Mon–Sat dinner

SA FOGANYA (€€)

Set above the harbour at Cales Fonts with an attractive interior patio, this restaurant specializes in charcoal grilled meat, fish and vegetables.
➕ L7 ✉ Carrer Ruiz y Pablo 93, Es Castell ☎ 971 354950 🕒 Lunch and dinner; closed Wed

SA LLIGA (€)

This bright, contemporary eatery has a terrace overlooking the port and is a great spot for a tapas lunch. The adjoining Club Maritimo restaurant offers silver service dining.
➕ e2 (fold-out map)
✉ Moll de Llevant 292, Maó

☎ 971 351372 🕒 Daily 8am–midnight

SA SARGANTANA (€)

Choose from tapas or a three-course lunchtime menu at this small restaurant, with tables outdoors on a covered terrace beside the Pont de Sant Roc bastion.
➕ b2 ✉ Plaça Bastió 14, Maó ☎ 971 362462
🕒 Lunch and dinner; closed Sun

SES FORQUILLES (€€)

www.sesforquilles.com
Trendy new-wave restaurant near the main square serving small portions of Mediterranean-Asian fusion food such as tuna sashimi, chicken and coconut curry, and asparagus in romesco sauce.
➕ b3 ✉ Sa Rovellada de Dalt 20, Maó ☎ 971 352711
🕒 Mon–Sat lunch, Thu–Sat dinner

FISH

The sea around Menorca is rich in fish and seafood, and there are working fishing ports at Fornells and Es Castell. Harbourside restaurants in Maó and Es Castell offer fresh squid, mussels, prawns, sole, sea-bass, bream, John Dory, tuna, swordfish and lobster, as well as rice-based dishes such as paella and 'black rice'. The most famous, and expensive, is *caldereta de llagosta*, spiny lobster soup from Fornells.

LA TROPICAL (€)

The locals come here for cheap, filling Spanish food, from breakfast, sandwiches and salads to tapas, pizza, paella, grilled meat and fish.
➕ b3 ✉ Carrer de la Lluna 36, Maó ☎ 971 360556
🕒 Lunch and dinner; closed Wed

VARADERO (€€€)

This fashionable restaurant on the harbourside specializes in fresh fish and rice dishes, as well as more unusual offerings such as duck breast in espresso and Guinness sauce.
➕ d2 (fold-out map)
✉ Moll de Llevant 4, Maó
☎ 971 352074 🕒 Lunch and dinner; closed Mon

VELL PARRANDER (€€€)

This small restaurant at the end of the promenade in Cales Fonts serves fresh fish, seafood paella and lobster from their own tanks.
➕ L7 ✉ Cales Fonts 52, Es Castell ☎ 971 369419
🕒 Lunch and dinner; closed Mon and Dec–Feb

VILLA MADRID (€€)

This Italian restaurant, serving fresh pasta dishes and wood-fired pizzas, is housed in a country house near the inland town of Sant Lluís.
➕ L7 ✉ S'Uestrà 46, Sant Lluís ☎ 971 150464
🕒 Sat–Sun lunch, Wed–Mon dinner

The eastern half of the island is pleasantly rural, with green meadows, stone walls and cattle farms. This area also contains several interesting Bronze Age sites, a charming fishing village, Menorca's highest mountain and its longest beach.

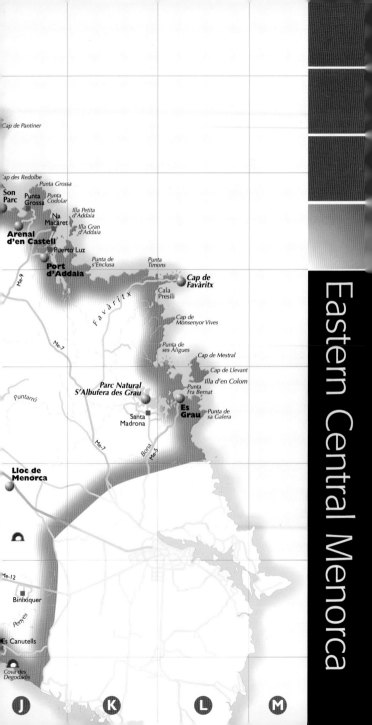

Cap de Pantiner

Cap des Redolbe

Punta Grossa

Son Parc

Punta Grossa

Punta Codolar

Na Macaret

Illa Petita d'Addaia

Illa Gran d'Addaia

Arenal d'en Castell

Puerto Luz

Port d'Addaia

Me-9

Punta de s'Enclusa

Punta Timons

Cap de Favàritx

Cala Presili

Favàritx

Me-7

Cap de Monsenyor Vives

Punta de ses Aligues

Cap de Mestral

Cap de Llevant

Illa d'en Colom

Parc Natural S'Albufera des Grau

Punta Fra Bernat

Puntarró

Santa Madrona

Es Grau

Punta de sa Galera

Me-7

Bona

Me-5

Lloc de Menorca

Me-12

Binixiquer

Penyes

Es Canutells

Cova des Degodadis

J K L M

Cales Coves

Cales Coves, with clear water for swimming (left) and prehistoric burial caves (right)

THE BASICS

+ H7
🍴 None
🚌 31 from Maó to Son Vitamina

DID YOU KNOW?

● Some of the finds from Cales Coves are on display at the Museu de Menorca (▷ 30).

TIP

● To explore inside some prehistoric burial caves, visit the necropolis at Cala Morell (▷ 100).

With a pair of pebble beaches joined by a cliff path and crystal-clear water for swimming, Cales Coves would be a special place even without the fascinating prehistoric burial caves which are carved into the rock.

Ancient necropolis The twin coves at Cales Coves are home to the largest Bronze Age necropolis in Menorca, with over 90 burial caves carved into the rock by hand. You get there by taking the rough dirt track marked 'Coves' from the township of Son Vitamina, just off the main road from Sant Climent to Cala En Porter. It is possible to negotiate this road by car but it is better to walk, a hike of around 2.5km (1.5 miles) down the Biniadris ravine. Arriving at the beach, the oldest caves are seen in the cliffs to your left, some of them dating back to the ninth century BC. Near here is a small freshwater spring, known to the ancient Romans who used Cales Coves as a port.

Modern troglodytes You can scramble over the rocks to your right to follow the cliff path to a second cove, where there are more modern caves built between the fourth century BC and Roman times. Although some served as burial chambers, others were used as dwellings, with decorated façades, door frames, windows, patios and niches. Some of them were still occupied until 2000, when the authorities evicted a group of squatters and modern-day cavemen. Access to the caves is now barred. Stay on the cliff path to climb to a viewpoint overlooking the cove.

Cap de Cavalleria

The lighthouse at Cap de Cavalleria (left) offers wide views of the coast (right)

Standing on this wild, lonely and wind-swept cape, it is easy to understand why Spanish author Carlos Garrido called it 'the end of the world...a supernatural landscape whose rocks almost groan with pain'.

Roman city Cap de Cavalleria is one of Menorca's wildest places, a remote headland at the northern tip of the island battered by the Tramuntana north wind. The Ecomuseu Cap de Cavalleria, in the old farmhouse of Santa Teresa, has exhibitions on the fauna, flora and history of the cape, mostly based on recent archaeological research. Although it is now virtually uninhabited, Cap de Cavalleria has a long history of human activity. In Roman times, this was the city of Sanisera, the third town on the island, with a thriving port at Sanitja. A short stroll from the museum down to the harbour passes the remains of a Roman basilica and military camp. Later, this was the site of Menorca's first mosque, the island's oldest lighthouse and a British defence tower.

Beaches and walks The ecomuseum issues a map of themed walking routes across the headland including walks for flora, fauna, beaches and stone quarries. A parking area gives access to the main beach, Platja de Cavalleria, with its long stretch of fine sand. From here, you can hike to more remote beaches or to the lighthouse, where there are views from the cliffs over the island of Illa dels Porros and the possibility of seeing nesting and migrant seabirds.

THE BASICS

✚ G1

Ecomuseu Cap de Cavalleria
www.ecomuseudecavalleria.com
✉ Finca de Santa Teresa, Camí de Sa Cavalleria
☎ 971 359999
🕐 Jul–end Sep daily 10–8.30; Apr–end Jun and Oct daily 10–7; closed Nov–end Mar
🍴 Café (€)
♿ Good
💷 Moderate

DID YOU KNOW?

● The mud in the cliffs at Cavalleria beach is believed to have healing properties—in summer you may see visitors rubbing it into their skin before sunbathing.
● The ecomuseum carries out underwater archaeological excavations each year, with volunteer divers exploring the seabed for evidence of the Roman city.

Fornells

HIGHLIGHTS

● Torre de Fornells
● Castell Sant Antoni
● Seafood restaurants
● *Caldereta de llagosta*

TIP

● You can go inside Torre de Fornells to see the old British ammunition stores and officers' quarters, then climb the spiral staircase to the roof for views over the north coast and Cap de Cavalleria (▷ 49).

There can surely be few more pleasant experiences in Menorca than strolling along the promenade in Fornells, taking your pick of the harbourside fish restaurants and dining on fresh lobster casserole beside the sea.

Fishing village This small fishing village of around 500 people is found on the west side of Port de Fornells, a deep natural harbour over 4km (2.5 miles) long which provides shelter for fishing vessels and yachts. Palm trees shade the waterfront promenade, and restaurants around the marina proudly display the catch of the local fishing fleet, including the spiny lobsters which go into the delicious *caldereta de llagosta* (▷ 68). The main thoroughfare, Carrer Major, set just back from the harbour, is a charming street of

Spend a relaxed day exploring the picturesque harbour (left) and streets of white-washed houses (right) in Fornells

whitewashed Mediterranean houses running between the harbourside square and the Church of Sant Antoni.

Fortress town Fornells played an important role in the defence of Menorca in the 17th and 18th centuries. The harbour was protected by Castell Sant Antoni, built in 1625 and modelled on Fort Sant Felip (▷ 37). The fort was destroyed by Spanish troops in 1782 but you can clamber over the ruins on a newly built walkway. Keep walking as far as the harbour mouth, where a path winds up the cliff face, passing the rock shrine of Ermita de Lourdes on its way to the Torre de Fornells. This circular watchtower was completed in 1802 during the final year of British rule and is the biggest of the defence towers around the Menorcan coast.

THE BASICS

➕ H2
🍴 Restaurants
🚌 From Maó and Es Mercadal

Torre de Fornells
🕐 Easter–early Apr and Oct Tue–Sun 9.30–3; early Apr–end Sep Tue–Sun 9.30–8.30, Sun–Mon 9.30–3; closed Nov–Easter
♿ None
💷 Inexpensive; free on Sun

Es Mercadal

TOP 25

TIP

● From the parking area beside the main road, walk through the underpass to reach the Centre Artesanal de Menorca, a crafts hub in the old barracks featuring displays by local artisans.

Sheltered beneath Monte Toro at the heart of Menorca, Es Mercadal makes a good place to break a journey across the island—particularly if you stop for lunch at one of its many excellent restaurants.

Market town Es Mercadal was founded in the 14th century as a market town midway between Maó and Ciutadella. Today, it is a sleepy town of whitewashed, green-shuttered houses with a reputation as a hub for traditional crafts and cuisine. From the outside, it is dominated by the church of Sant Martí and the 18th-century wind-mill, Molí des Racó, now a busy restaurant. The only real monument is the Aljub, reached by a flight of steps between the houses. This enormous cistern, built in 1735 on the orders of the British governor Sir Richard Kane, was designed to collect

The inland town of Es Mercadal, all whitewashed buildings with red roofs and green shutters, is surrounded by farmland and wooded hills

rainwater from the roof and channel it into a reservoir below. The cistern supplied drinking water not only to the local population but also to troops marching across the island.

Sweet treats Although it is now possible to travel from Maó to Ciutadella in under an hour, Es Mercadal still provides a pleasant refreshment stop along the way. In addition to its restaurants, the town has several pastry shops selling the traditional almond macaroons known as *amargos,* and the sugared almond cookies, *carquinyols*. The best-known manufacturer is Jaume Villalonga at Cas Sucrer, a master craftsman from the fourth generation of a family of confectioners dating back to 1873. He also produces *tortada* (almond cake), *pastissets* (cookies dusted with icing sugar), and caramels with dried fruit and nuts.

THE BASICS

➕ G4
🍴 Restaurants
🚌 1 from Maó and Ciutadella

Monte Toro

DID YOU KNOW?

● A monument in the courtyard recalls Father Pedro Camps (1720–90), a priest from Es Mercadal who founded the town of St. Augustine, Florida, in 1768. Descendants of some of the Menorcan's who first arrived with Father Camps still live in St. Augustine today.

TIP

● Before visiting the church, admire the views over the north coast from the terrace.

The pilgrimage to Monte Toro is well worthwhile if only for the views. From the summit, the island is laid out beneath you, with the sea on four sides and the mountains of Mallorca on the horizon.

Sacred mount At 357m (1,171ft), Monte Toro hardly qualifies as a mountain but it is the highest point on Menorca and the radar masts at its summit are visible from across the island. The name derives from *al-tor*, Arabic for a hill, but there is also a legend involving a *toro* (bull). The story is a variation of one which is told at numerous sacred sites in Spain. According to legend, a statue of the Virgin Mary was hidden in a cave during the Moorish occupation. Shortly after the Catalan conquest, the villagers were led by a bull to a cave at the summit of the mountain,

Clockwise from left: statue of the Black Madonna set into the altarpiece of the 17th-century church on Monte Toro; statue of Christ remembering the victims of a colonial war in Morocco; view over farmland from the summit of Monte Toro; ornately framed painting in the church; carved detail inside the church; exterior view of the church

where they discovered the statue. It was declared a miracle and the villagers built a shrine to house the statue. The chapel at Monte Toro is still a place of pilgrimage today.

The church A twisting road from Es Mercadal (▷ 52) leads to the summit, arriving beside an enormous statue of Christ with arms outstretched, honouring the victims of a colonial war in Morocco in the 1920s. Cross the courtyard and pass through a porch to enter the 17th-century church, all plain white walls beneath a central dome. A chapel contains the cave where the statue is said to have been found, along with farm tools used to bury it for protection during the Spanish Civil War. The statue itself is set into the altarpiece, a Black Madonna with a crown of precious stones and an effigy of the sacred bull at her feet.

THE BASICS

➕ H4
☎ 971 375060
🕓 May–end Oct daily 7am–8pm; Nov–end Apr daily 7–6
🍴 Café (€) and restaurant (€€)
♿ Good
🎫 Free

Parc Natural S'Albufera des Grau

Look out for waterfowl and nesting birds on a walk through the S'Albufera natural park, an area of marshland, forest, cliffs and sand dunes around a large freshwater lagoon. The park is the nucleus of Menorca's Biosphere Reserve.

Wetland paradise S'Albufera is the largest remaining wetland area in Menorca. Ducks, herons and cormorants can be seen on the lake, while osprey feed on the eels and mullet that thrive in its waters. The natural park encompasses a number of habitats, including forests of wild olive and holm oak, beaches, dunes, islets, cliffs and farmland. Although S'Albufera is now a nature reserve, its many resident species were seriously threatened in the 1970s, when developers planned to build a golf resort on the

Take a summer boat trip to Illa d'en Colom, seen here from the bay at Es Grau (left) or explore the Parc Natural S'Albufera des Grau on foot (right)

shores of the lake. The rejection of the plans was a turning point, as Menorca turned its back on uncontrolled tourism development in favour of preserving its natural heritage.

Visiting the park The best place to start is at the natural park reception building, which is signposted off the road from Maó to Es Grau (▷ 63), and where there is an exhibition on the ecology and wildlife of the park. A short walk from here leads to a parking area at the start of two waymarked trails. The green trail takes around 45 minutes and climbs high above the lagoon; the shorter red trail leads to a viewpoint overlooking the lake. The easiest walk is the blue trail, which begins near the entrance to Es Grau and follows a boardwalk between the lake and the dunes to emerge at the far end of the beach.

THE BASICS

✚ K5

✉ Carretera Maó-Es Grau

☎ 971 356303

🕐 Reception building May–end Oct Tue–Thu 9–7, Fri–Mon 9–3; Nov–end Apr daily 9–2

🍴 Cafés and restaurants at Es Grau

♿ Good

🆓 Free

Son Bou

Combine fifth-century history with a day on the beach at Son Bou

THE BASICS

➕ G6
🍴 Cafés and restaurants
🚌 From Maó in summer

DID YOU KNOW?

● It takes about an hour to walk along the beach to Sant Tomàs. It is possible to continue along the coast as far as Cala Santa Galdana (▷ 76).

TIP

● If the beach gets too crowded, keep walking west towards Sant Tomàs and you are bound to find a quieter spot–though you should be aware that the more secluded western end is popular with naturists.

The good, the bad and the ugly are found side by side on Menorca's longest beach, where the ruins of an ancient church lie hidden in the sand in the shadow of two huge modern hotels.

Golden beach The first sight of Son Bou is not promising, as the road passes through a rock tunnel and the view over the beach is dominated by twin high-rise hotels. This was one of Menorca's first tourist resorts, built in the days when big was beautiful and the environment was barely considered. Such architectural vandalism would never be permitted today. Yet stand with your back to the hotels and this is still a beautiful spot, with 3km (2 miles) of golden sand stretching all the way to Sant Tomàs (▷ 82). The eastern end of the beach, which gets crowded with sun-bathers in summer, has facilities ranging from beach bars to watersports. As you head west towards Sant Tomàs, the scenery becomes wilder, with sand dunes, marshes and paddy fields just behind the beach.

Seaside chapel A path behind the hotels leads to the ruins of a Christian basilica, dating from the fifth century. Not much remains of the original church, but look carefully at the pile of stones and you can see the outline of the triple nave as well as the baptismal font. From here you can climb onto the headland of Cap de Ses Penyes, where several ancient burial caves are carved into the cliff face. From the summit there are magnificent views along the south coast in both directions.

The ruins at Torralba d'en Salord echo with lives lived thousands of years ago

Torralba d'en Salord

As you wander around the remains of this prehistoric village, it only takes a little imagination to conjure up the lives of our ancestors—how they lived, how they died and how they worshipped.

Three millennia of occupation Although most of the buildings at Torralba d'en Salord date from the Talaiotic era, beginning around 2000BC, the settlement was also occupied in Roman and even medieval times. Excavations have revealed much about the Talaiotic lifestyle, in particular its ritual and religious nature. There is evidence of a bonfire having taken place in the horseshoe-shaped *taula* sanctuary and also an altar where a bronze figure of a horse was discovered. Other objects excavated here include a terracotta statue of the Punic goddess Tanit and a bronze figure of a young bull dating from the fifth century BC, which can both now be seen in the Museu de Menorca (▷ 30).

Exploring the ruins An easy-to-follow path leads around the site, with information panels and a leaflet helping you to understand the remains. The most impressive buildings are the two *talaiots*, built as watchtowers around 1300BC. The *taula* shrine is situated between them, with its central T-shaped *taula* monument intact. Details of everyday life can be observed in the grain silos carved out of the rock, the circular threshing floor and the hypogeum, an artificial cave used as a burial chamber. Finally there is a defensive wall and a hypostyle chamber, an underground gallery supported by columns which hold up the roof.

THE BASICS

✚ J6
✉ Carretera Alaior–Cala En Porter
☎ 696 217664
🕐 Jun–end Sep daily 10–8; Oct–end May Mon–Sat 10–1, 3–6
🍴 None
♿ None
👜 Moderate

HIGHLIGHTS

● *Talaiots*
● *Taula* sanctuary
● Hypostyle chamber

Torre d'en Galmés

HIGHLIGHTS

● Views over the south coast to Mallorca
● *Taula* sanctuary
● Hypostyle chamber
● Rainwater collection system

TIP

● This ancient site is accessible for wheelchairs and pushchairs–the main trail around the site is level but the *taula* sanctuary and lower village are harder to reach.

If you want to understand the Talaiotic culture of Menorca, Torre d'en Galmés is a good place to start. The Bronze Age village is easy to explore and offers the best introduction to prehistoric Menorca.

Opening up the past Until a few years ago, Menorca's ancient monuments were hidden away in the countryside, difficult to find but free to visit for anyone who made the effort. Today, one by one, they are being turned into tourist attractions. The result is that they are better maintained and easier to appreciate but some of the magic has been lost. The Talaiotic village at Torre d'en Galmés is perhaps the best example.

Getting there Start your visit at the interpretation building, just off the road from Alaior to Son Bou.

Surrounded by open countryside, the Talaiotic settlement of Torre d'en Galmés is a great place to gain an understanding of this ancient culture

Here you can see a film giving the background to the Talaiotic culture and visit a small museum with reproductions of objects from Torre d'en Galmés, including ceramic pots, a bronze helmet and a figure of Imhotep, an Egyptian deity, from the seventh century BC.

Exploring the ruins The actual site is found a short distance along the road. Follow the circular trail to climb to the highest point, whose central *talaiot* offers commanding views over the south coast. Nearby is the *taula* sanctuary, with the capital of the *taula* broken off. The lower part of the village, which is still being excavated, includes Talaiotic dwellings, a hypostyle chamber and an ingenious system of cisterns and channels cut into the rock for the collection and storage of rainwater.

THE BASICS

✚ H6

✉ Signposted off road from Alaior to Son Bou

🕐 Easter–early Apr and Oct Tue–Sun 9–3; early Apr–end Sep Tue–Sat 9–9, Sun 9–3; Nov–Easter free access

🍴 None

♿ Few

💶 Moderate; free on Sun and Nov–Easter

More to See

ALAIOR

The biggest of Menorca's inland towns appears from the main road as a cluster of white houses on a hill, crowned by the fortress-like church of Santa Eulària. The town was founded in 1304 by a royal charter issued by Jaume II of Mallorca, when he joined the parish of Santa Eulària to the nearby villages and the farmstead of Ilahor. Just downhill from the church, the 17th-century convent of Sant Diego is notable for its attractive cloister, set around a courtyard with white-washed walls and an old well in the middle. The cloister, known as Pati de Sa Lluna (Moon Courtyard), is being restored and there are plans for an ethnographic museum and concerts in the patio. Just 12km (7.5 miles) from Mawó, Alaior is a busy industrial town, best known as the hub of production of Mahón cheese. The Coinga factory (▷ 67), on the edge of town, has a wide range of cheeses for sale.

➕ H5 🍴 Restaurants 🚌 1 from Maó and Ciutadella

ARENAL D'EN CASTELL

This flourishing beach resort on the north coast has a glorious setting, high on the cliffs overlooking a horseshoe bay with an arena of fine sand. The beach itself shelves gently into the sea and is sheltered by the Punta Grossa headland. The resort has certainly suffered from overdevelopment and high-rise hotels mar the landscape, but it remains a popular spot for families, with good swimming and watersports in summer.

➕ J3 🍴 Restaurants 🚌 From Maó and Fornells in summer

CALA EN PORTER

The beach at Cala En Porter is typical of the south coast, set in a natural cove at the foot of a ravine and protected by tall limestone cliffs on either side. The western side is totally undeveloped, but the cliffs on the east side are now covered in hotels, villas and apartments. Its proximity to the airport means that this was one of the first holiday

The sandy bay at Arenal d'en Castell

A narrow street in old Alaior

resorts in Menorca. Most people come here for a drink in the cave bar, Cova d'en Xoroi (▷ below).

🔲 H7 🍴 Restaurants 🚌 31 from Maó

CAP DE FAVÀRITX

The lighthouse at Cap de Favàritx is a solitary beacon in a desolate landscape of black slate cliffs. On stormy days, when waves crash against the rocks and the wind almost knocks you off your feet, the cape has a savage beauty. Paths lead to the unspoiled beaches of Cala Presili, Cala Tortuga and Cala Morella Nou, inside the S'Albufera natural park (▷ 56).

🔲 L4

COVA D'EN XOROI

www.covadenxoroi.com

This famous bar and nightclub is located high in the cliff face, inside a natural cave with terraces overlooking the sea. The admission price during the day includes one drink. There is an interesting legend attached to the cave. The story goes that Xoroi, a Moorish pirate, was shipwrecked at Cala En Porter and took refuge in the cave. Meanwhile, a beautiful local girl disappeared on the eve of her wedding. Years later, following a rare snowfall, footprints in the snow led people to the cave where they found Xoroi and the girl living with their three children. On being discovered, Xoroi threw himself into the sea.

🔲 H7 ✉ Cala En Porter ☎ 971 377236 🕐 May–end Sep daily 11.30am–10.30pm, 11pm–5am; Mar–end Apr and Oct–end Nov Mon–Thu 11.30am–5.30pm, Fri–Sat 11.30am–10.30pm, 11pm–5am, Sun 11.30am–10pm; closed Dec–end Feb 🔲 None 🗖 Moderate

ES GRAU

The pretty fishing village of Es Grau is now a low-key holiday resort where many people from Maó have their summer homes. The wide sandy beach has shallow water for bathing and shelves gently into the sea, making it safe for children. A path behind the beach leads into the S'Albufera natural park (▷ 56). Boats make the journey in summer to the offshore

A hotel in Es Grau, attractively situated right on the bay

The famous Cova d'en Xoroi bar and nightclub

island of Illa d'en Colom, a former quarantine island, now uninhabited except for a rare species of lizard. The island has a pair of good beaches for swimming and sunbathing.

➕ L5 🍽 Restaurants 🚌 From Maó in summer

LLOC DE MENORCA

www.llocdemenorca.com

This small zoo, which opened in 2006, makes a good day out with children. The emphasis is on indigenous breeds of farm animals such as the Menorcan red cow, Mallorcan black pig and Menorcan sheep, goats and horses, but you can also see more exotic species including ostrich, emu, wallabies, parrots and lovebirds. During the winter months, the *porquetjades*, the traditional pig slaughter, takes place followed by the making of sausages.

➕ J6 ✉ L'Argentina, Alaior (on road from Maó to Ciutadella) ☎ 971 372403 🕐 May–end Sep daily 10–8; Oct–end Apr Tue–Sun 10–5 🍽 Café (€) 🚌 1 from Maó and Ciutadella ♿ Good 💷 Expensive

PORT D'ADDAIA

The long narrow inlet at Port d'Addaia provides perfect anchorage for yachts and the resort around the marina has become the haunt of visiting sailors. The British fleet landed here in 1798 during their final occupation of the island. The nearby seaside village of Na Macaret has an old-fashioned charm, with rows of white cottages facing a small sandy beach where the people of Alaior come at weekends.

➕ J3 🍽 Restaurants

SON PARC

The beach at Son Parc is one of the biggest on the island, in a magnificent bay backed by dunes and pine woods. Unfortunately, it has now been dwarfed by a sprawling and unsightly holiday resort, set around Menorca's only golf course (▷ 67). If you want some seclusion, follow the rocky coast path from the west end of the beach to the unspoiled cove at Cala Pudent.

➕ J3 🍽 Restaurants 🚌 From Maó and Fornells in summer

The beach at Son Parc is close to Menorca's only golf course

Port d'Addaia's harbour and resort are popular with sailors

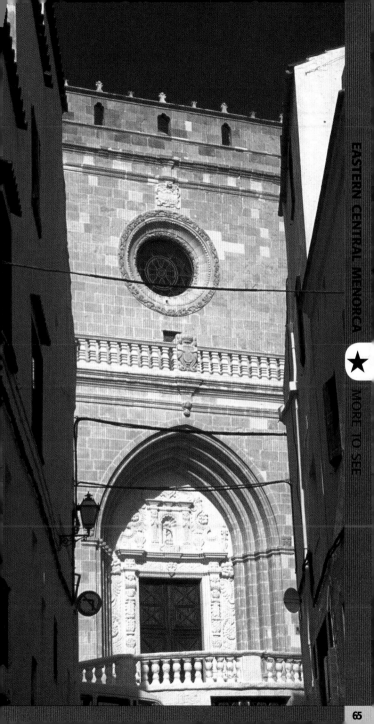

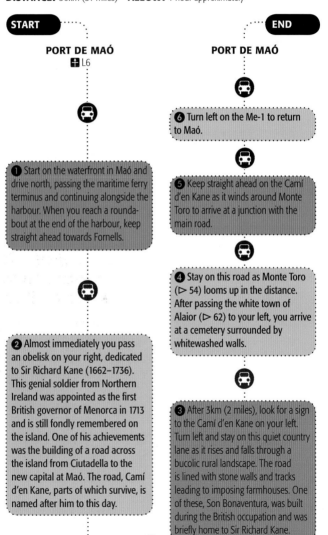

A Drive along Kane's Road

Enjoy peaceful rural scenery as you follow the old main road across the island, named after the first British governor of Menorca.

DISTANCE: 50km (31 miles)　**ALLOW:** 1 hour approximately

START

PORT DE MAÓ
➕ L6

❶ Start on the waterfront in Maó and drive north, passing the maritime ferry terminus and continuing alongside the harbour. When you reach a roundabout at the end of the harbour, keep straight ahead towards Fornells.

❷ Almost immediately you pass an obelisk on your right, dedicated to Sir Richard Kane (1662–1736). This genial soldier from Northern Ireland was appointed as the first British governor of Menorca in 1713 and is still fondly remembered on the island. One of his achievements was the building of a road across the island from Ciutadella to the new capital at Maó. The road, Camí d'en Kane, parts of which survive, is named after him to this day.

END

PORT DE MAÓ

❻ Turn left on the Me-1 to return to Maó.

❺ Keep straight ahead on the Camí d'en Kane as it winds around Monte Toro to arrive at a junction with the main road.

❹ Stay on this road as Monte Toro (▷ 54) looms up in the distance. After passing the white town of Alaior (▷ 62) to your left, you arrive at a cemetery surrounded by whitewashed walls.

❸ After 3km (2 miles), look for a sign to the Camí d'en Kane on your left. Turn left and stay on this quiet country lane as it rises and falls through a bucolic rural landscape. The road is lined with stone walls and tracks leading to imposing farmhouses. One of these, Son Bonaventura, was built during the British occupation and was briefly home to Sir Richard Kane.

Shopping

CENTRE ARTESANAL DE MENORCA

Opened in 2005 and housed in the old military barracks in Es Mercadal, the Centre Artesanal de Menorca has exhibitions of contemporary Menorcan handicrafts and a shop selling work by local artists. A craft garden features examples of rural Menorcan crafts including stone walls and carved olive-wood gates.

➕ G4 ✉ Recinte Firal, Es Mercadal ☎ 971 154436

COINGA

www.coinga.com
This cooperative of Menorcan dairy farmers is the largest producer

SAY CHEESE!
When buying Mahón cheese, remember that *tierno* is mild, *semicurado* is ripened for up to five months, while *curado* is fully flavoured and mature. The best farmhouse cheeses are labelled *artesano*, which means they are made by hand from unpasteurized milk and matured in olive oil.

of Mahón cheese. You can taste and buy the cheeses at the factory shop, and there are informative factory tours on Tuesday and Thursday at 11am.

➕ H5 ✉ Carretera Nova, Alaior ☎ 971 371227

SA FARINERA

www.safarineramenorca.com
Housed in a former flour mill which closed in 1999, this complex features gift shops, a restaurant and an industrial museum.

➕ G4 ✉ Carretera Maó–Ciutadella km20, Es Mercadal ☎ 971 154252

SUBAIDA

www.subaida.com
This farm shop offers visitors tastings of traditionally made Mahón cheese, and is found on the road north from Alaior towards the coast.

➕ H5 ✉ Camí de Binifabini, Alaior ☎ 971 368809

Entertainment and Activities

BOWLING SON BOU

In a large entertainment complex central to the resort, this American-style bowling alley is fun for adults and children alike.

➕ G6 ✉ Centro Comercial, Son Bou ☎ 699 017746 🕐 Apr–end Oct daily 4pm–late; Nov–end Mar Fri 7pm–2am, Sat 4pm–2am, Sun 4pm–11pm

COVA D'EN XOROI

www.covadenxoroi.com
This famous cave bar (▷ 63), open every night in summer for 'ambient sunset sessions', becomes a nightclub after 11pm.

➕ H7 ✉ Cala En Porter ☎ 971 377236 🕐 May–end Sep daily 11.30am–10.30pm, 11pm–5am; Mar–end Apr and Oct–end Nov Mon–Thu 11.30am–5.30pm, Fri–Sat 11.30am–10.30pm, 11pm–5am, Sun 11.30am–10pm; closed Dec–end Feb

GOLF SON PARC

www.golfsonparc.com
Menorca's only golf course opened in 1977 and has recently been extended to 18 holes, along with tennis courts and a driving range. Club rental is available,

and there are discounted rates for junior golfers.

➕ J3 ✉ Son Parc ☎ 971 359059 🕐 Summer daily 7–6; spring and autumn daily 9–5.30; winter daily 9am–dusk

MENORCA EN KAYAK

www.menorcaenkayak.com
Carlos and Maria Teresa offer sea-kayak rental, tuition and excursions in the S'Albufera natural park, including trips to remote beaches and the island of Illa d'en Colom.

➕ L5 ✉ Carrer S'Arribada 8, Es Grau ☎ 971 350069 🕐 All year

Restaurants

CA N'AGUEDET (€€)

This famous restaurant serves traditional island dishes such as home-cured sausages, rabbit with figs, and *oliaigua* (bread and olive oil soup). The owners produce their own wine.

✚ G4 ✉ Carrer Lepanto 30, Es Mercadal ☎ 971 375391 🕐 Daily lunch and dinner

CA N'OLGA (€€€)

An intimate restaurant in a 19th-century townhouse with a summer garden. The menu varies each season, with fresh local ingredients used to create both traditional Menorcan dishes and original Mediterranean cuisine. Desserts include home-made fig ice-cream. Reservations are recommended.

✚ G4 ✉ Carrer del Sol, Es Mercadal ☎ 971 375459 🕐 Jun–end Aug daily dinner; Apr–end May and Sep–end Oct hours vary; closed Nov–end Mar

ES CRANC (€€€)

It may not have the sea views but Es Cranc does have the freshest lobster in Fornells, delivered each day by local fishermen.

✚ H2 ✉ Carrer Escoles 31, Fornells ☎ 971 376442 🕐 Daily lunch and dinner; closed Nov–end Dec

CRANC PELUT (€€€)

At the start of the seafront promenade, Cranc Pelut serves some of the best seafood in Fornells, including razor clams, octopus meatballs and seafood casserole.

✚ H2 ✉ Passeig Marítim 98, Fornells ☎ 971 376743 🕐 Daily lunch and dinner; closed Nov–early Apr

MESÓN GALICIA (€€)

A taste of northern Spain in the heart of Menorca: fishy tapas and seafood specialties from Galicia.

✚ G4 ✉ Via Ronda 20, Es Mercadal ☎ 971 154098 🕐 Lunch and dinner; closed Mon

ES PLA (€€)

Romantic restaurant on the quayside at Fornells, with tables by the water's edge. Dishes such as *caldereta de llagosta* (▷ panel) and lobster sautéed in whisky are expensive, but there are lots of cheaper options.

✚ H2 ✉ Passeig Marítim, Fornells ☎ 971 376655 🕐 Daily lunch and dinner

CALDERETA DE LLAGOSTA

The classic dish of Menorca is *caldereta de llagosta*, a thick soup of spiny lobster from Fornells cooked with onion, garlic, tomato and parsley and served in an earthenware casserole. Expect to pay at least €70 per person; a cheaper alternative is *caldereta de peix i marisc*, made with fish and seafood instead of lobster.

SA LLAGOSTA (€€€)

This small, chic restaurant serves creative fish dishes such as cod with honey, tuna tartare and lobster with snails as well as the usual paellas and lobster casserole.

✚ H2 ✉ Carrer Gabriel Gelabert 12, Fornells ☎ 971 376566 🕐 Tue–Sat lunch and dinner, Sun lunch; closed Oct–end Mar

SA MITJA LLUNA (€)

The funky 'half-moon' café has sea-facing terraces and a simple menu of tapas, sandwiches and snacks.

✚ H2 ✉ Passeig Marítim 9, Fornells ☎ 971 376402 🕐 Jun–Sep daily 9am–2am; Apr–May and early to mid-Oct 9am–10pm; closed mid-Oct to Mar

TAST (€€)

Designer tapas and new-wave Mediterranean cuisine at a trendy restaurant with tables on the square. Unusual combinations include lamb sweetbreads with goat's cheese and wood-grilled octopus with bubble and squeak.

✚ G4 ✉ Plaça Pere Camps 21, Es Mercadal ☎ 971 375587 🕐 Lunch and dinner; closed Mon

The west side of the island is where Menorca's geological divisions become apparent. To the south, deep limestone gorges run down to the sea, while red sandstone predominates in the north. Several of Menorca's most beautiful unspoiled beaches are found in this area.

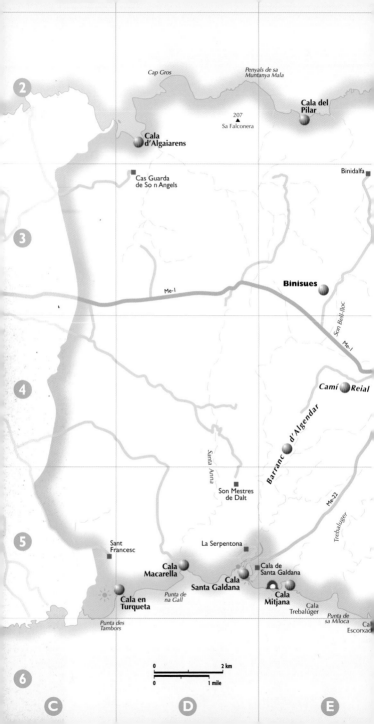

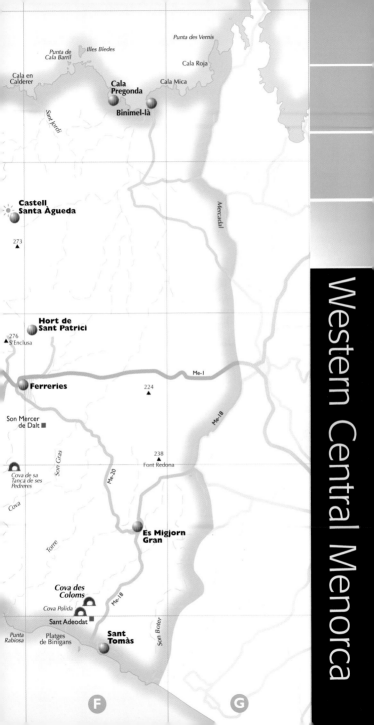

Punta des Vernis

Punta de
Cala Barril

Illes Bledes

Cala Roja

Cala en
Calderer

**Cala
Pregonda**

Cala Mica

Binimel·là

Sant Jordi

Mercadal

**Castell
Santa Àgueda**

273 ▲

**Hort de
Sant Patrici**

276
▲ S'Enclusa

Me-1

Ferreries

224
▲

Son Mercer
de Dalt ■

Son Gras

Me-20

238
▲
Font Redona

Me-18

Cova de sa
Tanca de ses
Pedreres

Cova

**Es Migjorn
Gran**

Torre

*Cova des
Coloms*

Me-18

Cova Polida

Sant Adeodat

*Punta
Rabiosa*

Platges
de Binigans

**Sant
Tomàs**

Son Boter

F   G

Binisues

The manor house at Binisues (left) displays 18th-century Menorcan aristocratic taste (right)

THE BASICS

🔲 E3
✉ Cami Ets Alocs
☎ 971 373728
🕐 May–end Oct daily 10–5; closed Nov–end Apr
🍴 Café (€) and restaurant (€€€)
♿ None
✋ Moderate

HIGHLIGHTS

● Walnut sideboard with stag's head in dining room
● Chippendale chairs in mirror salon
● Renaissance-style walnut writing desk in study
● Collection of stuffed birds and mammals
● Tool for gathering prickly pears in the old barn

A visit to the richly furnished manor house at Binisues will give you an insight into the lifestyle once enjoyed by Menorca's aristocratic families on their country estates.

Stately home The imposing mustard-painted farmhouse of Binisues stands at the heart of a large agricultural estate off the main road from Maó to Ciutadella. The 19th-century house still belongs to the descendants of the original owners and is approached by a grand driveway and a landscaped garden. Climb the stairs to the first floor to visit the family rooms, including the salon, drawing room, dining room, bedrooms, library and study. The rooms are lined with family portraits and filled with original 18th-century furniture in English, French and Spanish styles. The tastes of the Menorcan aristocracy were influenced by European fashions of the time and dark woods such as mahogany, cedar and cherry were in vogue. The study contains a fine walnut writing desk and embossed leather mahogany chairs.

The museum The second floor is devoted to the natural science collection of brothers Joan and Miguel Torrent, with display cases featuring over 200 species of Menorcan birds, mammals and reptiles and 1,000 species of butterflies and insects. You can also visit the old barn behind the house, with its collection of antique farm tools including ploughs, hoes, millstones, saddles and implements for picking and chopping prickly pears—as well as a 1928 Buick car.

The sands of Cala del Pilar are sheltered by dunes and low hills

Cala del Pilar

It might take a bit more effort to get to Cala del Pilar but it is worth it when you are greeted by the sight of a beautiful virgin beach sheltering beneath sand dunes and rocky outcrops.

Getting there Menorca has so many perfect beaches that even in high summer it is always possible to escape the crowds and seek out your own hidden cove. Cala del Pilar is not exactly a secret—the parking area is often full on summer weekends—but the effort involved in getting there means that it is never too crowded. Take the country lane signposted Camí Son Felip, just after the 34km post on the main road from Maó to Ciutadella. When the road runs out, leave your car and walk through the gate into the Alfurí de Dalt nature reserve. Follow the sandy path for about 30 minutes through a thick grove of oak and pine trees to emerge on the reddish sand dunes behind the beach. From here, it is easy to scramble down the rocks to the inviting wide sandy beach.

Beaches and coves A restored section of the Camí de Cavalls coast path continues from Cala del Pilar to Ets Alocs, an even more isolated cove. It is also possible to reach Ets Alocs by a rough track from the end of the road to Binisues (▷ 72) and Castell Santa Àgueda (▷ 78) and then approach Cala del Pilar along the cliffs. At the opposite end of Cala del Pilar, a path leads over the headland to Macar d'Alfurinet, with its strange beach of giant pebbles.

THE BASICS

➕ E2
🍴 None

DID YOU KNOW?

● The freshwater spring at Cala del Pilar is guarded by a small figure of Our Lady of Pilar.
● The red sand on the beach is said to have therapeutic properties for the skin.

TIP

● The walk through the woods is tiring and there are no facilities when you arrive, so make sure you take plenty of water with you.

Cala Macarella

● It is also possible to walk to Cala Macarella along the coast path from Cala En Turqueta (▷ 80), following a clifftop trail with magnificent views over the south coast.

Try to imagine the perfect Mediterranean beach and you will probably be thinking of Cala Macarella. With pine-scented cliffs, clear turquoise water and soft white sand, this is one of the most idyllic spots on the Menorcan coast.

Virgin beach When the Menorcans talk about 'virgin' beaches, they mean places like Cala Macarella. Formed by a cleft in the cliffs where a deep gorge enters the sea and hemmed in by tall limestone crags to either side, the cove at Macarella is typical of the south coast. Pine trees reach almost to the water, providing welcome shade on sunny days, and the sea is warm, shallow and clear. This picturesque spot has long been appreciated and the prehistoric burial caves in the cliffs on the west side of the beach now

A coast path stroll (left) will lead you to the idyllic Mediterranean coves of Cala Macarella and Cala Macarelleta (right)

act as summer homes for locals. There is even a beach bar, Café Susy, offering showers and lunchtime snacks.

Getting there Although it is possible to drive there on a rough track from Ciutadella, the best way to approach Cala Macarella is on the cliff path from Cala Santa Galdana (▷ 76). The well-marked trail across the headland takes around 30 minutes, with several paths leading off to *miradors* overlooking the coast. Eventually you arrive at a long wooden staircase which drops down to the beach. For greater seclusion, take the path behind the beach leading through the woods to the twin cove of Cala Macarelleta, where nudist bathing is permitted. A separate path climbs high onto the cliffs to a viewpoint where you can look down over both beaches at once.

THE BASICS

✚ D5
🍴 Café Susy (€)

TIP

● Arriving by car, follow the signs from the Ciutadella ring road and leave your car in the free parking area, from where it is a 15-minute walk to the beach. In summer, electronic boards along the road from Ciutadella will tell you if the parking is full.

Cala Santa Galdana

It may have grown into one of Menorca's biggest holiday resorts, but Cala Santa Galdana retains enough of its beauty to see why the locals refer to it as the island's most spectacular bay.

Summer playground In July or August, when the beach is crowded with sunbathers and there is barely room to lay your towel on the sand, you might think that Cala Santa Galdana was nothing more than souvenir shops, bars, pizzerias, pedal boats, waterslides, mini-golf courses and ice-cream stands. The resort has become so popular that at times it is difficult to appreciate its natural beauty: Set in a wide horseshoe bay where the Barranc d'Algendar (▷ 80) flows into the sea, this is a rare example in Menorca of a beautiful spot spoiled by thoughtless development. The unsightly hotels

Left to right: the sometimes crowded beach at Cala Santa Galdana; hotel complexes overlook the small marina; outdoor dining in the shade of the palm trees in Cala Santa Galdana's popular resort

dominating the cliffs would almost certainly not be permitted today.

Queen of the coves   It is a different story if you visit out of season. The beach is deserted and there are peaceful walks in the riverside park at the start of the Barranc d'Algendar. When the park runs out, climb the steps beside a gate to walk inland along the gorge, alive with butterflies, birds and wild flowers. As the river enters the sea, it widens to form a small pleasure harbour for boats. A footbridge crosses the stream to El Mirador restaurant, on a rocky promontory overlooking the beach. Climb the steps at the east end of the beach to Mirador de Sa Punta, a clifftop lookout with views over the bay. A nearby path threads through the woods to the unspoiled beaches at Cala Mitjana (▷ 81) and Cala Mitjaneta.

THE BASICS

✚ D5

🍴 Lots of cafés and restaurants

🚌 51 from Maó; 52 from Ciutadella; 53 from Ferreries in summer

DID YOU KNOW?

● Older people recall the days when Cala Santa Galdana was an unspoiled cove, and access involved a donkey cart ride along a rough track from Ferreries.

Castell Santa Àgueda

The views from Santa Àgueda (left) are worth the climb up the old Roman road (right)

THE BASICS

- ✚ E3
- 🍴 None
- ♿ None
- 💲 Free

DID YOU KNOW?

- The ruined chapel at the summit was built after the Catalan conquest and dedicated to Santa Àgueda (St. Agatha).
- According to legend, before the Arabs surrendered the castle, they threw down loaves of bread on their Christian conquerors as a sign of their resistance.

TIP

- It is a steep climb of about 30 minutes to reach the summit, so take plenty of water and wear good walking shoes.

The views from the top of Menorca's third highest hill will take your breath away—if you have any breath left after the steep climb to the summit on an old Roman road.

The Moors' last stand Today it stands in ruins, but the castle at the summit of Santa Àgueda was at one time the most powerful fortress on the island. The Romans had a fort here but most of what you see remaining today dates from the period of Arab occupation. The Moorish rulers of Menorca strengthened the fort, adding square and round towers and surrounding the entire complex with a defensive wall. Although it is now abandoned and overgrown, with a little imagination it is possible to picture the castle as it was in 1287, as Alfons III of Aragón chased the Moorish armies across the island and they retreated to their stronghold to make their last desperate stand.

Getting there The path to the summit begins beside an old schoolhouse on the Binisues road. Follow this road for 3km (2 miles) and leave your car near the white entrance gates to Santa Cecilia farm. The track is rough at first but soon gives way to an old Roman road, with cobblestone paving zigzagging its way to the top. From a height of 264m (866ft), there are extensive and magical views over the north and west coasts. You should be able to make out Monte Toro (▷ 54), the lighthouses at Cap de Cavalleria and Cap d'Artrutx, and the mountains of Mallorca on the horizon.

Taste Mahón cheese at this museum and shop which also sells wine and other local fare

Hort de Sant Patrici

On a visit to this farmhouse museum near Ferreries, learn about the history and production of Mahón cheese before indulging yourself with free samples of the island's most famous product.

Family farm The manor house at Hort de Sant Patrici, now a small rural hotel, was built in 1919 in the Palladian style as a summer house for Menorcan painter Fernando Vives. Today it belongs to the Casals family. The extensive grounds contain vineyards, a sculpture garden and a modern bodega, but the real reason for visiting is to learn about Mahón cheese.

The visit The self-guided audiotour begins with a stroll through the gardens before heading up to the dairy. On weekday mornings, you may be able to see workers moulding and pressing the cheese. There is evidence of cheesemaking in Menorca as far back as 3000BC but the origins of Mahón cheese date from the import of Friesian cattle under British rule in the 18th century. The cheese was awarded its own denomination of origin in 1985 and is now officially known as *Queso de Mahón-Menorca*. The best farmhouse cheeses are made using unpasteurized milk, wrapped in cotton and cured with olive oil. At the cheese museum, inside an old barn, you see shelves of ripening cheeses as well as vintage wooden milk churns and a cheese press carved from a wild olive tree. Afterwards, you can visit the shop for tastings of Mahón cheese; it also sells local wines, liqueurs, sausages, pastries and jams.

THE BASICS

www.santpatrici.com

➕ F4

✉ Camí de Sant Patrici s/n, Ferreries

☎ 971 373702

🕐 May–end Oct Mon–Sat 9–1.30, 4.30–8; Nov–end Apr Mon–Fri 9–1, 4–6, Sat 9–1

🍴 None

♿ Good

📷 Moderate

DID YOU KNOW?

● The sculpture trail was created in 2003 at a symposium held to celebrate the 10th anniversary of Menorca's Biosphere Reserve. In the middle is *Los Amantes* by Eduardo Cruz, a pair of entwined lovers symbolizing the relationship between humanity and nature.

More to See

BARRANC D'ALGENDAR

The deepest and most dramatic of Menorca's limestone gorges runs for 6km (4 miles) from Ferreries to the south coast. The stream on the valley bed flows throughout the year, feeding lush gardens and orchards before emptying into the sea at Cala Santa Galdana (▷ 76). Unfortunately it is not possible to walk the entire length of the gorge, though there is limited access at both ends. From the beach at Cala Santa Galdana, follow the riverside footpath then climb the steps beside a gate to continue along the valley floor. Approaching from Ferreries, follow the Camí Reial (▷ 81) to its end or take Camí Barranc d'Algendar from the main road to arrive at a parking area beside the Algendar Vell youth hostel. From here, you can continue on foot between limestone cliffs. A popular folk song, *Sa Nuvia d'Algendar*, tells the tale of a young bride from Algendar who was captured by Moorish pirates on the day of her wedding.

🔖 E4

BINIMEL·LÀ

This large beach of red sand and dunes is notable for its freshwater lake. It is also the start of a 20-minute walk to Cala Pregonda (▷ 81).

🔖 F2 🍴 Restaurant (€) in summer

CALA D'ALGAIARENS

These twin beaches on the north coast have recently been opened up as part of a government campaign to provide road access to Menorca's virgin beaches. The road from Ciutadella passes through La Vall, a fertile region of farmland, oak and pine woods. Both beaches have golden sand, clear water and peaceful views.

🔖 D2 🍴 None

CALA EN TURQUETA

This beautiful south coast beach can be reached by road from Ciutadella, though parking is a 20-minute walk uphill from the beach. It is possible to walk along the cliffs from here to Cala Macarella (▷ 74).

🔖 D5 🍴 None

A hillside village in the Barranc d'Algendar

The beach at Binimel·là

CALA MITJANA

The twin coves of Cala Mitjana and Cala Mitjaneta are easily accessible by road or by way of a 30-minute walk from Cala Santa Galdana (▷ 76). The main beach at Cala Mitjana shelters beneath pine woods and cliffs dotted with caves.

➕ E5

CALA PREGONDA

A 20-minute walk from the west end of Binimel·là (▷ 80) leads to this sheltered bay, named after the offshore sandstack which is said to resemble a praying monk. The path crosses salt flats and climbs up to a headland before dropping down to the sandy beach at Pregondó and continuing to Cala Pregonda. The combination of golden sand, crystal-clear water, pine woods and dunes makes this one of the most tranquil spots on the north coast. Out of season you might have this place to yourself, but despite its remoteness it is popular with locals in summer.

➕ F2 🍴 None

CAMÍ REIAL

The Camí Reial (Royal Road) was a medieval cart track linking Ciutadella to Maó. A small section of the road near Ferreries has now been restored and opened as a footpath. The route begins in the middle of Ferreries and continues for 3.5km (2.2 miles) across rolling countryside to the head of the Barranc d'Algendar (▷ 80). Along the way, you pass Sa Cova Reial, a cave used as shelter by shepherds and farmers, and probably at one time as a prehistoric dwelling.

➕ E4

COVA DES COLOMS

This vast, eerie limestone cave, the size of a cathedral, is hidden away inside the Barranc de Binigaus. It can be reached on foot by following the path through the gorge from Es Migjorn Gran (▷ 82).

➕ F5

FERRERIES

Menorca's highest town is named after the blacksmiths who once

The golden sand and clear water of the sheltered bay at Cala Pregonda

The huge limestone cave in the Barranc de Binigaus known as Cova des Coloms

worked here, though today it is better known as a centre for the manufacture of leather shoes. The oldest part of town is based around the church square, where the handsome town hall faces the 19th-century parish church of Sant Bartomeu. Downhill from here, Plaça d'Espanya is the venue for a lively craft and farmers' market on Saturday mornings. Ferreries is also the starting point for the walk along the Camí Reial (▷ 81). Just outside Ferreries, off the road to Es Migjorn Gran, is the prehistoric village of Son Mercer de Baix, where the remains of Talaiotic houses and a burial naveta are situated at the confluence of two ravines.

🔲 E4 🍽 Cafés and restaurants 🚌 1 from Maó and Ciutadella

ES MIGJORN GRAN

The sleepy village formerly known as San Cristóbal is inland Menorca at its best—white houses with green shutters and cream-coloured window frames along a single main street which comes alive briefly in the

mornings before dozing during the afternoon siesta. There is a village bar, a couple of decent restaurants and a doll's-house parish church, and views over the countryside down to the coast. The village lies at the heart of the migjorn, the southern half of the island with its fertile farmland, deep valleys and limestone cliffs. A popular walk leads down to the sea through the Barranc de Binigaus (▷ 83).

🔲 F5 🍽 Café and restaurants 🚌 71 from Maó; 72 from Ciutadella

SANT TOMÀS

With a boardwalk promenade running behind a long sandy beach, Sant Tomàs is one of Menorca's more attractive resorts. The main beach is a continuation of that at Son Bou (▷ 58). At the west end of the resort, a path leads to the quieter beaches of Sant Adeodat and Binigaus, the latter of which is popular with naturists.

🔲 F6 🍽 Cafés and restaurants 🚌 71 from Maó; 72 from Ciutadella in summer

Ferreries hosts a bustling craft and farmers' market on Saturday mornings

Es Migjorn Gran's main street

Barranc de Binigaus

This limestone gorge walk from Es Migjorn Gran to the coast has dramatic scenery, ancient monuments and a spectacular cave.

DISTANCE: 7km (4.5 miles) **ALLOW:** 3 hours

START

ES MIGJORN GRAN
✚ F5 🚌 71, 72

1 Begin on the road to Sant Tomàs and turn right on Avinguda David Russell, signposted 'Cova des Coloms'. Leave your car outside the school at the end of this road.

2 Turn left to walk along the lane, with a large *talaiot* visible in the field to your left. Pass a cemetery on your left and keep straight ahead passing a second *talaiot* on your right. Passing the farmhouse of Binigaus Vell, you crest a hill and have your first view of the sea.

3 Stay on the lane as it continues downhill. When you reach a junction of paths, keep ahead towards Platja de Binigaus.

4 At the entrance gates to Binigaus Nou, turn left through a gap in the wall signposted 'Platja de Binigaus'. The path descends steeply into the gorge.

END

ES MIGJORN GRAN

7 Return to the signpost and turn right to climb out of the valley. When you reach the lane, turn right to return to Es Migjorn Gran.

6 Retrace your steps to the well and the junction of paths. Turn right and stay on this path as it climbs up the gorge. After 30–40 minutes, you reach a signpost (broken at the time of writing). Turn right to scramble up the path to Cova des Coloms (▷ 81).

5 Eventually you reach a junction of paths with yellow arrows pointing the way. Take the right fork towards the beach. The path climbs high above the valley with views to the far side. When you reach a well, follow the track to Binigaus beach.

Shopping

CA'N DOBLAS
www.candoblas.com
This small workshop facing the church in Ferreries sells traditional Menorcan *abarcas* (leather sandals) by master craftsman Joan Doblas Camps, who set up the business with his grandfather in 1983. In addition to classic styles, there are 'fantasy' sandals for women and funky hand-painted designs for kids.
🔳 F4 ✉ Plaça Jaume II 1, Ferreries ☎ 971 155021

HORT DE SANT PATRICI
www.santpatrici.com
Even if you don't want to visit the museum

(▷ 79), this farm shop near Ferreries sells locally produced cheese and wine, as well as specialty foods and wines from the other Balearic islands.
🔳 F4 ✉ Camí de Sant Patrici s/n, Ferreries ☎ 971 373702

JAIME MASCARÓ
www.jaimemascaro.com
This factory outlet on the main road near Ferreries sells shoes by Jaime and Ursula Mascaró, whose celebrity clients include Claudia Schiffer and Lily Allen. Mascaró is best known for ballet shoes but the range also includes high heels, boots, handbags and men's shoes.
🔳 F4 ✉ Poligon Industrial, Ferreries ☎ 971 373837

Entertainment and Activities

AUDAX SPORTS & NATURE
To experience the great outdoors, head for the hut on the promenade beneath the Hotel Audax at Cala Santa Galdana. Activities include horse riding, scuba diving, fishing, tennis and hire of mountain bikes, kayaks and canoes. There is also a three-hour kayak excursion into the caves at Cala Mitjana, a bike ride to remote south coast beaches, and guided walks in the Barranc d'Algendar (▷ 80) and Barranc de Binigaus.
🔳 D5 ✉ Passeig del Riu, Cala Santa Galdana ☎ 971 154548 ⏰ Apr–end Oct

SON MARTORELLET
www.sonmartorellet.com
The show at Son Martorellet combines equestrian arts, ballet, music, acrobatics and circus skills to provide an enjoyable evening for adults and children. The emphasis is on Menorcan horses, with riders in aristocratic costume getting them to prance and rear on their hind legs just as they do at traditional island fiestas. The stables are open to visitors during the day, with guided tours of the farm and occasional mini-shows. It is situated just outside Ferreries on the road to Cala Santa Galdana.
🔳 E4 ✉ Carretera Cala Galdana, Ferreries ☎ 639 156851 ⏰ May–end Oct Tue and Thu 8.30pm; stables May–end Oct Mon–Sat 10–1, 3–8

♫ ENTERTAINMENT AND ACTIVITIES

Restaurants

58 S'ENGOLIDOR (€€)

www.sengolidor.com

A charming old family house, on the main street of Es Migjorn Gran, is now a small hotel and restaurant specializing in traditional Menorcan cuisine. Classics include cheese soufflé, fish casserole and skate with garlic and capers. In summer, you can dine on the terrace with views over the valley.

➕ F5 ✉ Carrer Major 3, Es Migjorn Gran ☎ 971 370193 🕐 May–end Jun and Oct Sat–Sun lunch, Tue–Sun dinner; Jul–end Sep Tue–Sun dinner; closed Nov–end Apr

BAR PERI (€)

A typical village bar on the main square of Es Migjorn Gran, serving traditional tapas such as meatballs, *tortilla* and spicy potatoes.

➕ F5 ✉ Sa Plaça 1, Es Migjorn Gran ☎ 971 370115 🕐 Daily lunch and dinner

BINISUES (€€€)

The stately manor house at Binisues (▷ 72) has an excellent restaurant specializing in Menorcan country cooking and fish dishes, such as lobster casserole and crayfish

with beans. Another specialty is *greixera*, a traditional dessert of eggs, bread and Mahón cheese cooked in a clay pot.

➕ E3 ✉ Camí Ets Alocs ☎ 971 373728 🕐 Lunch and dinner; closed Sun

CAFÉ SUSY (€)

The beach bar at Cala Macarella is just the place for a lunchtime snack of cured ham, grilled squid or roast chicken beside the sea.

➕ D5 ✉ Cala Macarella ☎ 971 359467 🕐 May–end Oct daily 10–6; closed Nov–end Apr

EL GALLO (€€)

This rustic farmhouse restaurant on the road to Cala Santa Galdana has a vine-shaded terrace and wood-beamed interior decorated in Menorcan folk style. Charcoal grills are the specialty, from

rabbit with *allioli* (garlic mayonnaise) to steak with Mahón cheese.

➕ F4 ✉ Carretera Cala Galdana, Ferreries ☎ 971 373039 🕐 Lunch and dinner; closed Mon and Dec–end Jan

LIORNA (€€)

www.liorna.com

Hidden away in the back streets of Ferreries, this new-wave restaurant and art gallery is worth seeking out. Pizzas are cooked in a wood oven and include unusual offerings like goat's cheese with spinach and dates. Other specialties are risotto, salads and anglerfish with *cuixot* sausage, apples and vanilla.

➕ F4 ✉ Carrer Ecònom Florit 9, Ferreries ☎ 971 373912 🕐 Fri–Sun lunch, Tue–Sun dinner

MIGJORN (€€€)

Set in a 17th-century house with a palm-shaded garden at the entrance to the village, this restaurant offers creative Mediterranean cooking, using local Menorcan produce in unexpected ways. The signature dishes include lamb stew with liquorice, skate with black pudding and French toast with camomile ice-cream.

➕ F5 ✉ Avinguda de la Mar 1, Es Migjorn Gran ☎ 971 370212 🕐 May–end Jun and Sep–end Oct Fri–Sun dinner; Jul–end Aug Thu–Tue dinner; closed Nov–end Apr

Ciutadella, Menorca's second city, is a town of palaces and churches with an air of aristocratic dignity which dates back to its original status as island capital. Nearby attractions include several good beaches and the well-preserved ancient burial chamber of Naveta des Tudons.

Ciutadella and the West

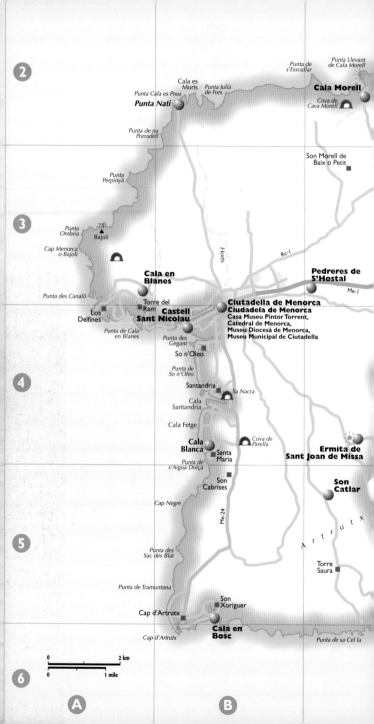

2

Punta de
s'Esscullar

Cala es
Morts   Punta Llevant
                         de Cala Morell
Punta Cala es Pous   Punta Julià
Punta Nati   de Fors   **Cala Morell**

                                      Cova de
                                      Cava Morell

Punta de na
Porradell

Son Morell de
Baix o Petit

3

Punta
Perpinyà

Punta   75
Ombria   ▲
             Bajoli

Cap Menorca
o Bajoli   Rc-1

             Cala en
             Blanes   **Pedreres de**
                                           S'Hostal
Punta des Canaló
                 Torre del   Me-1
Los   Ram
Delfines   **Castell**   **Ciutadella de Menorca**
               Sant Nicolau **Ciudadela de Menorca**
                              Casa Museu Pintor Torrent,
Punta de Cala   Catedral de Menorca,
en Blanes   Punta des   Museu Diocesà de Menorca,
              Gegant   Museu Municipal de Ciutadella
              So n'Oleo

              Punta de
              So n'Oleo
              Santandria   Sa Nacra

4
              Cala
              Santandria

              Cala Fetge
                          Cova de
              Cala   Parella
              Blanca   **Ermita de**
              Santa   **Sant Joan de Missa**
              Maria
              Punta de
              s'Aigua Dolça
                                      Son
              Son   **Catlar**
              Cabrises

Cap Negre
                   Me-24
                                      A r t r u t x
5
Punta des
Sac des Blat

                                      Torre
Punta de Tramuntana   Saura

              Son
              Xoriguer
Cap d'Artrutx

Cap d'Artrutx **Cala en**
               Bosc   Punta de sa Cel la

0   2 km
0   1 mile

6

A   **B**

Punta de
Fra Bernat

Cova d'en
Guardia

Coves des
Pinar des Tudons

**Naveta des
Tudons**

**Arenal de
Son Saura**

Punta
des Pinar

C   D   E

Ciutadella

HIGHLIGHTS

- Catedral (▷ 97)
- Museu Diocesà (▷ 98)
- Museu Municipal (▷ 98)
- Plaça des Born
- Ses Voltes

DID YOU KNOW?

- Plaça de S'Esplanada is commonly known as Plaça dels Pins because of the pine trees which grow there. At the other end of the old town, Plaça d'Alfons III is known as Plaça de Ses Palmeres because of its palms.

It was an 18th-century governor of Menorca, the Count of Cifuentes, who captured the essence of Ciutadella when he famously observed that 'Maó may have more people, but Ciutadella has more souls.'

Catalan capital When the British moved the capital to Maó, the Catholic church stayed behind in Ciutadella and the noble Catalan families refused to abandon their Gothic palaces and townhouses. Even today, the former capital has a stately, historic feel, along with a strong artistic temperament. As you wander around the old town, keep an eye out for architectural details, from hidden courtyards and fountains to coats of arms carved in stone. At the same time, Ciutadella is a lively, modern city with open-air cafés, art

Clockwise from left: harbourside in Ciutadella's Old Town; sculpted detail and tower on a building on Plaça des Born; sun-drenched buildings around Plaça des Born; the arched hallway and staircase of Ciutadella's Palau Salord; bronze sculpture on a road junction; twin balconies decorating Ciutadella's stone cathedral

galleries and trendy boutiques in the maze of narrow streets around the cathedral.

Streets and squares The main square, Plaça des Born, is surrounded by handsome buildings, including a pair of 17th-century palaces with Italianate loggias and a 19th-century theatre. The obelisk in the middle commemorates the city's resistance to a Turkish raid in 1558. The crenellated town hall stands on the site of the former governor's palace. Climb the steps behind the town hall to the remains of Bastió d'es Governador, a fortress with views over the port. From Plaça des Born, Carrer Major des Born leads to the cathedral and the pedestrian-only streets of the old town, including Ses Voltes, with old-fashioned shopfronts and cafés beneath a row of whitewashed Moorish arches.

THE BASICS

➕ B4
🍴 Cafés and restaurants
🚌 1 from Maó

TIP

● Take a leisurely stroll along Passeig Marítim, a wide seafront promenade between Cala d'es Degollador and the port. The views are magnificent, particularly at sunset from Castell de Sant Nicolau (▷ 97).

Naveta des Tudons

DID YOU KNOW?

● Before its excavation in the 1950s, the *naveta* was used by local farmers as a cattle shed.

TIP

● Visit on a Sunday morning, when entrance is free, or late on a summer evening when you might have the monument to yourself.

Of all Menorca's prehistoric monuments, this is probably the most impressive—a Bronze Age burial chamber in the shape of an upturned boat which has stood in a field outside Ciutadella for over 3,000 years.

Navetas The ancient Talaiotic people of Menorca built *talaiots* for protection and *taulas* for ritual purposes but they also needed somewhere practical to bury their dead. The caves around the Menorcan coast were used as resting places, but purpose-built *navetas,* whose name derives from their shape, resembling an upturned boat are also found. These huge structures were built from colossal stones, held together without mortar by the same technique which is still used on the island to build dry-stone walls.

The entrance (left) to the Naveta des Tudons (right), a Bronze Age burial chamber, is approached through a gap in the dry-stone wall that surrounds the whole monument

Visiting the monument The Naveta des Tudons is the oldest and largest surviving burial *naveta* on Menorca, dating from around 1000BC. Clearly visible from the main road from Maó to Ciutadella, it is reached by a short walk from the parking area across the fields. The building is 7m (23ft) high and 14m (46ft) long, with a horseshoe ground plan, a rounded apse and a small entrance at its western end. Access to the entrance is now barred but it is possible to peer inside. A small corridor leads to the main burial chamber, built on two levels, one of which probably acted as an ossuary for bones. The remains of more than 100 bodies have been found here, together with personal ornaments such as bracelets, necklaces, bronze pendants and ceramic pots. Some of the items from the burial hoards are now on display at the Museu de Menorca (▷ 30).

THE BASICS

✚ C3
✉ Carretera Maó-Ciutadella, km40
🕐 Easter–early Apr and Oct Tue–Sun 9–3; early Apr–end Sep Tue–Sat 9–9 (or sunset if earlier), Sun–Mon 9–3; Nov–Easter free access
🍴 None
♿ None
💷 Inexpensive; free on Sun and Nov–Easter

Pedreres de S'Hostal

If you have never thought of visiting a disused quarry, then think again—this former industrial site near Ciutadella has been transformed into one of the island's most unexpected and special places.

Marés Marés (sandstone) has been used as a building material in Menorca ever since the ancient Talaiotic people built the nearby Naveta des Tudons (▷ 92). Found across the southern half of the island, the white stone is still used in the construction of houses today. The sandstone quarry at S'Hostal was among the largest on the island and was in operation for 200 years before closing for business in 1994. It has now been opened to visitors as a unique tourist attraction, with walking trails, sculptures, labyrinths and botanical gardens inside the old quarries.

Clockwise from top left: the restful medieval garden hidden deep in the old quarry; the deep, sheer walls of the modern quarry, which closed for work in 1994; nature is beginning to reclaim this former industrial site; try your luck in the labyrinth

On the trail You need to allow an hour to follow the clearly marked trail around the site. The path leads first into the old quarry, where stone was extracted by hand using hammer and chisel. Shady trails lead beneath stone walls into hidden gardens of Mediterranean plants. Eventually you arrive at the medieval garden, with orchards, herb gardens, rose bushes and a cool sandstone fountain at its heart.

Sandstone cathedral The second half of the trail takes you deep inside the modern quarry, where you stand beneath the sheer white walls of a sandstone cathedral, 30m (98ft) deep and dramatically carved out of the rock. The quarry is watched over by *Totem*, a sculpted sandstone figure 5m (16ft) tall, discovered in the old quarry and now the symbol of S'Hostal.

THE BASICS

www.lithica.es

🞥 C3

✉ Camí Vell km 1, Ciutadella

☎ 971 481578

⊙ Mid-Mar to mid-Oct Mon–Sat 9.30–dusk (Jul–end Aug closed 2.30–4.30), Sun 9.30–2.30; mid-Oct to mid-Mar Mon–Fri 9.30–2.30, Sat–Sun 9.30–dusk

🍴 None

⛔ Few

💵 Moderate; free in winter

Son Catlar

*Rebuild Son Catlar in
your imagination to
gain an understanding
of Talaiotic village life*

THE BASICS

➕ C5
✉ On road from Ciutadella
to Arenal de Son Saura
🕐 Free access
🍴 None
♿ None
🎫 Free

DID YOU KNOW?

● Defensive walls like the
one at Son Catlar are known
as Cyclopean because of
the belief that they must
have been built by a race
of giants.

**It may not have the immediate appeal of
some of Menorca's other ancient sights,
but a walk around Son Catlar is the best
way to get a feel for the layout of a
Talaiotic village.**

The village Son Catlar is the largest surviving
prehistoric village on Menorca, and the only one
still to be surrounded by its original wall. Research
shows that the village grew to its present size
in the second century BC and continued to be
occupied until the last years of Roman rule.
Much of the site has yet to be excavated and the
monuments are in a poor state of repair, but it is
still possible to appreciate the size and complexity
of this ancient settlement.

Around the walls At the entrance to the
village, you pass a hypogeum, an underground
burial chamber hewn out of the rock. From here,
you can make a complete circuit of the defensive
rampart, some 870m (2,850ft) in length and
constructed out of massive Cyclopean stones with
a series of square towers added in Roman times.
It is easy to imagine how the wall would have
provided security for the prehistoric inhabitants.
Soon you arrive at the north gate, the only surviving entrance to the village, topped by a giant lintel.
After making the circuit of the wall, follow the path
into the village, passing the remains of Talaiotic
houses on your way to the *taula* sanctuary in the
middle. Sheep graze beneath wild olive trees and
crumbling *talaiots* blend into the landscape in this
atmospheric and peaceful spot.

More to See

Ciutadella

CASA MUSEU PINTOR TORRENT

www.casatorrent-menorca.com

This small museum in Ciutadella is dedicated to local artist José Torrent (1904–90), who lived and worked in this house near Plaça des Born. His daughter Margarita runs the museum and you may be shown around by his grandchildren. The collection features paintings from throughout his life, from realist Menorcan landscapes to later experiments with Impressionism and Expressionism.

✚ B4 ✉ Carrer Sant Rafel 11, Ciutadella ☎ 971 380482 🕓 Jun–end Oct Mon–Sat 11–1, 7.30–9.30, Sun 8–9.30pm; Nov–end May Fri, Sat 7pm–9pm ♿ Good 🎟 Free

CASTELL DE SANT NICOLAU

This 17th-century watchtower at the mouth of Ciutadella's port stands at the midway point of the Passeig Marítim. Crowds gather here on summer evenings to watch the sunset, with the mountains of Mallorca silhouetted against a pink sky. A statue on the promenade commemorates David Glasgow Farragut (1801–70), the son of a Ciutadella emigrant who rose to become First Admiral of the US Navy.

✚ B4 ✉ Plaça Almirall Farragut, Ciutadella ☎ 971 381050 🕓 Tue–Sat 11–1, 6–8 ♿ None 🎟 Free

CATEDRAL DE MENORCA

Although Maó has been the administrative capital of Menorca since 1713, Ciutadella remains the religious capital. The cathedral was constructed shortly after the Catalan conquest on the orders of the victorious Alfons III, and it rose on the site of what had been the island's main mosque. Built in Catalan Gothic style, it was desecrated by Turkish pirates in 1558 and partially destroyed during the Spanish Civil War, so the present cathedral has been heavily restored.

✚ B4 ✉ Plaça de la Catedral, Ciutadella ☎ 971 380739 🕓 Daily 9–1, 6–9 ♿ Good; separate entrance on Carrer de Ca'l Bisbe 🎟 Free

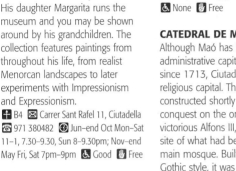

Tres Madres (Three Mothers) *by José Roberto Torrent Prats, on display at the Casa Museu Pintor Torrent in Ciutadella*

Nave of the Catedral de Menorca in Ciutadella

MUSEU DIOCESÀ DE MENORCA

www.bisbatdemenorca.com

The Diocesan Museum occupies a former Augustinian monastery beside the church of Església dels Socors. The galleries are arranged around the cloister, a peaceful garden with a well at the centre and a collection of 15th-century gargoyles from the cathedral. Archaeological exhibits include a bronze figure of a Siren (half-woman, half-bird) discovered in a cave at Es Mercadal (▷ 52), and a Roman statuette depicting a slave with a rope around his neck. There is also a gallery of paintings by Pere Daura (1896–1976), a Catalan artist born in Ciutadella who married American painter Louise Blair and settled in the United States after World War II. They include portraits of his wife and daughter, and an Impressionist view of the harbour at Maó. The former monks' refectory, just off the cloister, is notable for its vaulted ceiling. It is also worth going inside the church to see the 18th-century frescoes covering the dome and walls.

🚩 B4 ✉ Carrer del Seminari 7, Ciutadella ☎ 971 481297 ⏰ May–end Oct Mon–Sat 10.30–2; closed Nov–end Apr 🚻 None 💷 Inexpensive ❓ Free admission to cloister May–end Oct Mon–Sat 4–7pm

MUSEU MUNICIPAL DE CIUTADELLA

Housed in the Bastió de Sa Font, a 17th-century fortress overlooking the harbour, the Municipal Museum details the early history of Menorca from Talaiotic to Roman and Islamic times. Highlights include Roman coins, jewellery and dice, lead and stone ammunition used by the famed Balearic slingshot throwers, and skulls from the Talaiotic era showing evidence of primitive brain surgery.

🚩 B4 ✉ Plaça de Sa Font, Ciutadella ☎ 971 380297 ⏰ May–end Sep Tue–Sat 10–2, 6–9; Oct–end Apr Tue–Sat 10–2 🚻 None 💷 Inexpensive; free on Wed

The West

ARENAL DE SON SAURA

On summer weekends the people of Ciutadella head for the unspoiled

The neoclassical entrance to the Museu Municipal de Ciutadella

The unspoiled beach at Arenal de Son Saura

beaches of the south coast and this is one of the best. As a result of the government campaign to reclaim public access to Menorca's beaches, you can now drive all the way to Son Saura and there is a large parking area behind the beach. After leaving the car walk left through the pine woods to the wide sandy beach, or right to a series of rocky coves. Arenal de Son Saura can also be reached on the coastal footpath from Son Xoriguer to Cala Santa Galdana.
➕ C5 🍴 None

CALA BLANCA

Cala Blanca is the furthest south in a cluster of beach resorts which are gradually being swallowed up into Ciutadella. The main attraction here is the beautiful beach, which offers visitors clear turquoise water beneath limestone cliffs and the remains of a Bronze Age *naveta* hidden among the pines. Further north are the smaller beaches at Cala Santandría and Sa Caleta, separated by an old watchtower on a cliff.

➕ B4 🍴 Cafés and restaurants 🚌 64 from Ciutadella in summer

CALA EN BLANES

What was once a succession of narrow creeks to the west of Ciutadella has become a sprawling mega-resort of villas, apartments and foreign pubs. At the heart of the resort is Aquacenter (▷ 103), Menorca's biggest waterpark. To get away from it all, walk along the cliffs to Pont d'en Gil, a natural rock arch with spectacular sea views.
➕ A3 🍴 Cafés and restaurants 🚌 61 from Ciutadella in summer

CALA EN BOSC

This chic resort at the southwest tip of Menorca nestles around its marina, separated from the sea by a narrow artificial channel. The busy harbourside is lined with restaurants and bars. Boards by the harbour advertise boat trips to remote south coast beaches in summer. The biggest beach is in the nearby resort of Son Xoriguer, a popular

A restaurant terrace overlooks the water at Cala Blanca

The marina is at the heart of the resort of Cala en Bosc

hub for watersports including scuba diving and windsurfing. At sunset, people gather on the cliffs near the lighthouse at Cap d'Artrutx for views across the sea to Mallorca. Coastal footpaths lead north to the beach resort of Cala Blanca (▷ 99) and west to beautiful Arenal de Son Saura beach (▷ 98).

B5 Cafés and restaurants 65 from Ciutadella in summer

CALA MORELL

The main reason for visiting Cala Morell is to clamber over the Bronze Age necropolis, in a series of caves dug out of the cliff face around 1000BC. It is possible to climb right inside the caves, some of which feature columns and decorative façades. Although they were originally built as burial chambers, the caves were later adapted for living purposes. The necropolis was even used in the 20th century as a holiday resort for Spanish workers.

C2 Cala Morell Free access None Free

ERMITA DE SANT JOAN DE MISSA

This 15th-century Gothic chapel, surrounded by countryside on the road to the south coast beaches, is charming in its simplicity. The small whitewashed church has great symbolic value to the people of Ciutadella as this is where the members of the traditional brotherhoods ride on horseback on the eve of the festival of Sant Joan (23 June) for a blessing from the bishop.

C4 Camí de Sant Joan de Missa Mon 4–7pm Good Free

PUNTA NATI

The rocky, barren landscape to the north of Ciutadella is deserted apart from the presence of numerous *ponts.* These dry-stone sheep and cattle shelters, up to seven tiers high, could easily be mistaken for ancient *talaiots.* A narrow road leads to a lighthouse, standing all alone on the cliffs. This is the start of the bike ride to Cap d'Artrutx (▷ 101).

B2

The simple but locally important Ermita de Sant Joan de Missa

Explore the Bronze Age burial caves at Cala Morell

The Lighthouse Route

Enjoy sea air and views on a gentle bike ride between two lighthouses. Bikes can be hired from Velos Joan, Ciutadella (▷ 102).

DISTANCE: 16km (10 miles) **ALLOW:** 1 hour 30 minutes

START

PUNTA NATI
✛ B2

1 Start by the lighthouse at Punta Nati in the far northwest of the island and follow the country lane to Ciutadella across a lonely landscape dotted with stone *ponts* (sheep shelters).

2 Reaching the ring road, cross the roundabout carefully and keep straight ahead for Ciutadella. Fork right to follow the one-way system, then turn left to pass around the head of the port. Turn right alongside the Museu Municipal (▷ 98) and stay on Carrer de Sa Muradeta to reach Plaça des Born.

3 Keep right around the square and turn right beside the town hall, then right again on Camí de Baix. This brings you out above the port. Pass the yacht club and continue around the seafront promenade to its end.

END

CAP D'ARTRUTX
✛ B6

6 After passing the entrance sign for Cap d'Artrutx, turn right along Passeig Marítim. Follow this road along the cliffs to arrive by the lighthouse at Cap d'Artrutx.

5 Stay on this road as it rises and falls through typical Menorcan countryside. The road can get busy in summer, so be sure to stay on the wide cycle path.

4 Turn right at Platja Gran beach following signs to Sa Caleta and keep ahead at a second roundabout. Stay on this road until you reach a junction by the Blanc Palace hotel. Turn left to cycle through the resort area of Sa Caleta. When you reach a roundabout, turn right towards Cap d'Artrutx, passing a turn-off to Cala Santandría on your right.

Shopping

BLAU MARÍ
This shop off Plaça des Born sells bright summer clothing, including organic cotton T-shirts, skimpy dresses and decorative Menorcan sandals for adults and children.
➕ B4 ✉ Carrer Major des Born 11, Ciutadella
☎ 971 481095

BON GUST
A classy delicatessen on the main pedestrian shopping street, selling Menorcan cheese, sausages, wine and gin.
➕ B4 ✉ Carrer de Maó 20, Ciutadella ☎ 971 484414

CA NA FAYAS
This delicatessen on the inner ring road specializes in Mahón cheese, with several varieties of farmhouse cheese on sale at better prices than elsewhere. Ask to taste before you buy.
➕ B4 ✉ Avinguda Conqueridor 47, Ciutadella
☎ 971 381686

CA SA POLLACA
This lovely old shop beneath the arches has been selling shoes since 1897. There is a good selection of *abarcas,* traditional Menorcan sandals, and espadrilles in a wide variety of designs.
➕ B4 ✉ Ses Voltes 23, Ciutadella ☎ 971 382223

ES CELLERET DE CA'S COMTE
Situated below street level in the vaults of the 19th-century Torre-Saura palace, this delicatessen and wine cellar offers tastings of Menorcan wine and Mahón cheese. It also sells a wide range of local produce, including *sobrasada,* a spicy pork sausage flavoured with red pepper.
➕ B4 ✉ Carrer Major des Born 6, Ciutadella
☎ 971 385009

JOYERÍA CARLES
One of the best of the many shops selling jewellery in the narrow streets of the old town.
➕ B4 ✉ Carrer Santa Clara 16, Ciutadella
☎ 971 380734

PATRICIA
This Ciutadella designer is one of the leading manufacturers of men's and women's shoes in Menorca, as well as bags, leather jackets and other fashions. In addition to the Carrer Seminari boutique, there is another branch on the steps leading down to the port and a factory outlet on the outskirts of town on the road to Cala Santandría.
➕ B4 ✉ Carrer Seminari 40, Ciutadella ☎ 971 385205

SA FIDEUERA
The former pasta factory beside the market has been turned into a trendy wine bar and delicatessen which sells pasta, sausages, ham, cheese and wine.
➕ B4 ✉ Carrer Castell Rupit 24, Ciutadella ☎ 971 386451

SES INDUSTRIES
This small shop in the back streets of Ciutadella has shelves lined with bottles of Menorcan and Spanish wines, brandy, liqueurs and cheese in olive oil.
➕ B4 ✉ Carrer Santa Clara 4, Ciutadella ☎ 971 382882

VELOS JOAN
Whether you just want to ride around town or follow the lighthouse route from Punta Nati to Cap d'Artrutx (▷ 101), at this bike shop in the middle of town you can rent bikes and scooters by the day. City bikes, mountain bikes and tandems are available.
➕ B4 ✉ Carrer Sant Isidre 32, Ciutadella ☎ 971 381576

MERCAT DE CIUTADELLA
Ciutadella's central market occupies an attractive 19th-century arcade on Plaça de la Llibertat, whose shopfronts are decorated with green and white decorative tiles. Stalls sell fresh vegetables, local sausages and Mahón cheese, and there are several cheap cafés and bars nearby. A separate building, dating from 1895, houses the fish market, selling fresh fish from the island's fishing ports. The market is open Monday to Saturday mornings.

Entertainment and Activities

AQUACENTER

www.aquacenter-menorca.com
This waterpark in the heart of Cala En Blanes has plenty of thrills and spills for all the family, including the Black Hole, Adventure River, waterslides and children's pools. There are also trampolines, bouncy castles and a play area for younger children.
🔲 A3 ⊠ Avinguda Principal urb. Los Delfines, Cala En Blanes ☎ 971 388251 ⏰ May–end Oct daily 10–6.30

AQUAROCK

www.aquarockmenorca.com
A small waterpark at Cala En Bosc with pools, wave machines and the Kamikaze waterslide. The same complex includes Karting Rock, a go-kart track.
🔲 B5 ⊠ Carrer Cova d'es Moro, Cala En Bosc ☎ 971 387822 ⏰ May–end Oct daily 10.30–6 (go-karts 10.30am–10.30pm)

ASERE

Salsa bar and club by the harbour, where Latin sounds keep clients happy into the early hours. It's popular with the locals because it stays open throughout the year.
🔲 B4 ⊠ Port de Ciutadella ☎ 659 988397 ⏰ Summer daily 6pm–5am; winter Fri–Sat 6pm–5am

CERCLE ARTÍSTIC

www.cercleartistic.com
The 19th-century coffee house on Plaça des Born is home to a cultural institution founded in 1881, whose activities include the Menorca Symphony Orchestra and a folklore group. Concerts take place in the downstairs auditorium or in the splendid municipal theatre situated next door.
🔲 B4 ⊠ Plaça des Born 19, Ciutadella ☎ 971 385753

HIPODROM DE CIUTADELLA

www.hipodromdeciutadella.com
Popular trotting races take place at this racetrack from 6pm on Sunday evenings, with the jockey sitting in a small cart behind the horse. To join in the fun, have a bet on the horses.
🔲 A3 ⊠ Torre del Ram, Cala En Blanes ☎ 971 388038 ⏰ Mar–end Nov Sun 6pm

JAZZBAH

www.jazzbahclub.com
This bar behind the harbour has live music most weekends, and is popular with local bands as a venue for promoting their new albums. The music is an eclectic mix of jazz, blues and rock. The downstairs bar can get crowded but there is an open-air terrace on the upper level.
🔲 B4 ⊠ Pla de Sant Joan 3, Ciutadella ☎ 971 482953 ⏰ Jun–end Sep daily 11pm–4am; Oct–end May Fri–Sat 11pm–4am

SA CLAU

www.saclau.com
Intimate jazz and cocktail bar inside a natural cave by the harbour. You may be able to catch some live jazz here on Friday nights in summer.
🔲 B4 ⊠ Port de Ciutadella ☎ 971 384863

SURF & SAIL MENORCA

www.surfsailmenorca.com
Watersports centre on the beach at Son Xoriguer offering windsurfing, catamaran and dinghy sailing, either on your own or with an instructor. Other activities include water-skiing, wakeboarding and high-speed rides in a two-person 'donut' or eight-person inflatable 'banana boat'. You can also hire a catamaran or motorboat to explore the remote south coast beaches.
🔲 B5 ⊠ Platja Son Xoriguer, Cala En Bosc ☎ 971 387105

SUMMER NIGHTS

The hub of Ciutadella nightlife is Pla de Sant Joan, the large open space behind the marina. On summer nights, this area is buzzing as young people gather at its terrace bars and clubs. The musical styles vary from place to place, so it is easy to find something to suit your taste. Popular choices include Jazzbah, Sa Kova and La Vela, which opened in an old warehouse in 2008.

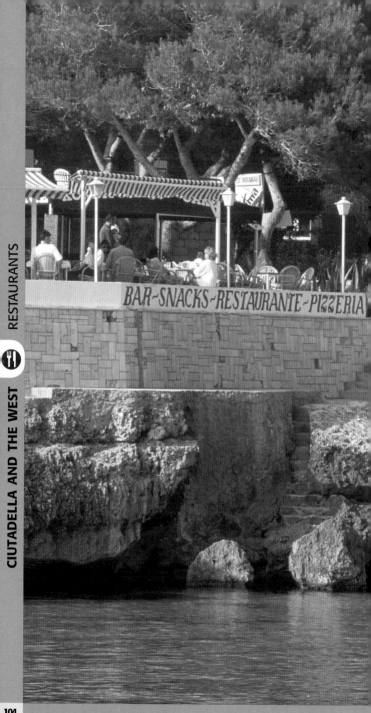

BAR~SNACKS~RESTAURANTE~PIZZERIA

Restaurants

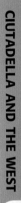

PRICES

Prices are approximate, based on a 3-course meal for one person.

€€€	over €40
€€	€20–€40
€	under €20

CAFÉ BALEAR (€€)

www.cafe-balear.com
Seafood restaurant in a great location by the harbour, with tables on the waterfront where the fishermen bring in their catch. Lobster, mussels, swordfish and John Dory are on the menu, fresh from the restaurant's own fishing boat. The set lunch menu is excellent value.
🚩 B4 ✉ Passeig Es Pla De Sant Joan 15, Ciutadella ☎ 971 380005 🕐 Daily lunch and dinner

CA'N BEP (€€)

Traditional high-end dining in a 1935 townhouse with an art nouveau façade and a conservatory lined with *azulejo* tiles. The menu includes fresh fish, paella, lobster and steaks.
🚩 B4 ✉ Passeig Sant Nicolau 4, Ciutadella ☎ 971 487815 🕐 Lunch and dinner; closed Tue

CAN LLUÍS (€€)

This small restaurant in the back streets of Ciutadella specializes in *bacalao* (salt cod), which is served in a variety of ways—with honey, garlic, *allioli* (garlic mayonnaise),

leeks or *escalivada* (roasted vegetables).
🚩 B4 ✉ Carrer Alaior 22, Ciutadella ☎ 971 380154 🕐 Lunch and dinner; closed Sun

CA'S CÒNSOL (€€)

With a balcony overlooking the port from the top of the medieval walls, this restaurant has the best view in Ciutadella. The food is Mediterranean with Moroccan touches, including hummus, vegetable couscous and Agadir-style sardines.
🚩 B4 ✉ Plaça des Born 17, Ciutadella ☎ 971 484654 🕐 Lunch and dinner; closed Sun

CA'S FERRER DE SA FONT (€€€)

Housed in an old blacksmith's forge dating from 1756, Ca's Ferrer offers fresh interpretations of Menorcan classics, including home-made

MENÚ DEL DÍA

Most restaurants offer a *menú del día* at lunchtime, which is a great way of eating a filling meal at a reasonable price. The daily set menu is chalked up on a blackboard, with three or four choices for each course. The price typically includes starter, main course and dessert with wine or water for between €10 and €20—less than you might otherwise pay for a main course.

sausages, roast suckling pig and a burger made from pig's trotters.
🚩 B4 ✉ Carrer Portal de Sa Font 16, Ciutadella ☎ 971 480784 🕐 Sep–end Jun Tue–Sun lunch, Thu–Sat dinner; Jul–end Aug Mon–Sat lunch, daily dinner

LA CAYENA (€)

Offbeat wine and tapas bar in an old townhouse with stone walls, arches and Moroccan tiled tables. The name means 'the pepper' and the menu features spicy options such as *fajitas*, curries and stir-fries, as well as Mediterranean food.
🚩 B4 ✉ Carrer Alaior 40, Ciutadella ☎ 971 482212 🕐 Summer Mon–Sat lunch and dinner; winter Fri–Sat dinner

FUSION CAFÉ (€)

This trendy bar on the promenade is popular with a young crowd. The menu features everything from burgers to tofu, salads to sandwiches and gazpacho to guacamole. There are sea views from the terrace and occasional live music at weekends.
🚩 B4 ✉ Carrer Ruiz i Pablo 78, Ciutadella ☎ 971 381332 🕐 Daily lunch and dinner

EL JARDÍ (€€)

www.restaurantesjardi.com
Set in the pretty courtyard garden of the Hostal Oasis, El Jardí serves contemporary Spanish

cuisine alongside traditional meat and fish dishes. Lighter touches include seafood, vegetarian dishes and strawberry soup in summer.

➕ B4 ✉ Carrer Sant Isidre 33, Ciutadella ☎ 971 480516 🕐 Daily lunch, Mon–Sat dinner

ORISTANO (€€)

Named after Ciutadella's twin town in Italy and set in an old factory overlooking the port, Oristano specializes in pizza, cooked in a traditional wood-fired oven. Unusual varieties include Bombay pizza (chicken curry, pineapple and banana). The menu also features fresh pasta, roast lamb, smoked octopus, steak with pistachio, and liquorice ice-cream for dessert.

➕ B4 ✉ Carrer Francesc de Borja Moll 1, Ciutadella ☎ 971 384197 🕐 Summer daily 7pm–1am; winter Thu–Sun 7pm–1am

PA AMB OLI (€€)

Paradise for carnivores and a nightmare for vegetarians—steaks, barbecued meat, ostrich, rabbit with crab. The house special is *pa amb oli* (bread with olive oil and tomato) served with ham, cheese or *escalivada* (roasted vegetables).

➕ B4 ✉ Carrer Nou de Juliol 4, Ciutadella ☎ 971 383619 🕐 Lunch and dinner; closed Sun

ES PUNTET (€€€)

www.espuntet.es
Fashionable designer restaurant beneath the arches on Ses Voltes, offering ultra-modern fusion food with Asian and Mediterranean touches. The menu varies according to season but might include venison with shitake mushrooms and couscous, or cod croquettes in fig sauce.

➕ B4 ✉ José Maria Cuadrado (Ses Voltes) 24, Ciutadella ☎ 971 484863 🕐 Tue–Sun lunch, Tue–Sat dinner

ROMA (€)

Excellent pizzas cooked in a wood oven, plus fresh pasta and grilled meat at this pizzeria, part of the Café Balear chain.

➕ B4 ✉ Carrer Alcàntara 18, Ciutadella ☎ 971 384718 🕐 Lunch and dinner; closed Sun

---

VEGETARIANS

There is little tradition of vegetarian cooking in Spain, but it is possible to avoid meat and fish and still eat well in Menorca. Tapas bars (▷ 86) serve *tortilla* and other snacks, including garlic mushrooms and e*scalivada* (roasted vegetable salad). Pizza and pasta are reliable choices, and most restaurants serve excellent salads. Another good standby is *pa amb oli*, bread with olive oil, tomato and Mahón cheese.

SA QUADRA (€€)

Inside a natural cave behind the beach at Cala Santandría, Sa Quadra offers traditional Menorcan cuisine with unexpected touches. Alongside classic dishes like lobster casserole, grilled fish and shoulder of lamb, the menu also features hake with blackberries, pork with plums, wild boar with truffles, and duck leg with chocolate and balsamic vinegar. Desserts are home-made and might include chocolate brownie with white chocolate sauce and mandarin sorbet, cheese flan with candied figs or almond tart with vanilla ice-cream. There is also a separate children's menu.

➕ B4 ✉ Platja Santandría 16, Ciutadella ☎ 971 480 959 🕐 May–end Oct daily 12–12; closed Nov–end Apr

ES TAST DE NA SILVIA (€€)

This restaurant beside the marina at Cala En Bosc offers sophisticated Spanish cuisine by chef Silvia Anglada. The menu includes specialties such as oysters in *cava*, duck breast with Pedro Ximenez, and salt cod with pears and blue cheese. There is also a good-value lunchtime set menu.

➕ B5 ✉ Avinguda Portixol 21, Cala En Bosc ☎ 971 387895 🕐 Summer Thu–Tue lunch and dinner; winter Sat–Sun lunch

Menorca has many accommodation options, from high-rise beach hotels to self-catering apartments and a growing number of rural hotels. Most rooms are reserved by tour operators in summer, so independent visitors need to plan ahead and book well in advance.

Introduction

With over 95 per cent of visitors arriving between April and October, accommodation in Menorca is seasonal in nature. Hotels in Maó, Ciutadella and the inland towns stay open all year, but most beach resorts shut down in winter and many hotels only open in the first week of May.

Countryside or coast?

The majority of hotel rooms are found on the coast, in resorts such as Arenal d'en Castell, Cala Santa Galdana and Son Bou. Hotels here tend to be booked up by tour operators in summer, with the best deals available as part of a package holiday. If you plan to stay on the coast, you need to book well in advance, particularly during the peak season of mid-June to mid-September. An alternative is to stay inland in one of the growing number of small rural hotels, several of which are included in the listings on the following pages.

Hotel or apartment?

Another alternative is to search online for a self-catering villa or apartment. This will give you a greater sense of privacy and the freedom to cook your own meals. This option is particularly suitable for families or groups of friends. At the upper end of the scale, some villas have their own private gardens and pools.

Prices

Hotel prices vary according to season, rising to a peak in July and August. The best deals are available in April, May and October. Rates quoted generally include breakfast but exclude 7 per cent IVA (VAT).

Menorca has a choice of accommodation including waterside apartments, city hotels and rural retreats

SIX OF THE BEST

- Best budget hotel: Hostal Fornells (▷ 109)
- Best for city breaks: Casa Albertí (▷ 110)
- Best for honeymooners: Biniarroca (▷ 112)
- Best rural retreat: Sant Joan de Binissaida (▷ 112)
- Best seaside hotel: Hotel Port Ciutadella (▷ 111)
- Best spa hotel: La Quinta (▷ 112)

Budget Hotels

58 S'ENGOLIDOR

www.sengolidor.com
A village house in Es Migjorn Gran which has been converted into a small restaurant and hotel. Four cosy rooms are individually decorated with local furniture, art and antiques, plus an attic suite with its own living room and bathroom.
🔢 F5 ✉ Carrer Major 3, Es Migjorn Gran ☎ 971 370193 🕐 Apr–Oct

HOSTAL CIUTADELLA

www.alojarseenmenorca.com
Good budget hotel in the old town of Ciutadella and close to the market. 17 rooms.
🔢 B4 ✉ Carrer Sant Eloy 10, Ciutadella ☎ 971 383462 🕐 All year

HOSTAL FORNELLS

www.hostalfornells.com
Located on the main street of Fornells, with a decent sized pool in the garden. There's also a café and bar on site. 17 rooms.
🔢 H2 ✉ Carrer Major 17, Fornells ☎ 971 376676 🕐 May–Oct

HOSTAL JENI

www.hostaljeni.com
This old-style hotel in Es Mercadal has recently been given a refreshing update with the addition of a terrace garden, sauna and heated pool with retractable roof. The restaurant at Hostal Jeni is famous for its traditional Menorcan cuisine. 56 rooms.
🔢 G4 ✉ Mirada del Toro 81, Es Mercadal ☎ 971 375059 🕐 All year

HOSTAL OASIS

A charming oasis in the heart of Ciutadella, with nine simple rooms around a pretty courtyard garden.
🔢 B4 ✉ Carrer Sant Isidre 33, Ciutadella ☎ 971 382197 🕐 May–Oct

HOSTAL LA PALMA

www.hostallapalma.com
Small hostel on the harbourside square

in Fornells, with a swimming pool in the garden. 25 rooms.
🔢 H2 ✉ Plaça S'Algaret 3, Fornells ☎ 971 376634 🕐 Apr–Oct

HOSTAL S'ALGARET

www.hostal-salgaret.com
Old-style hostel with 22 rooms, all with balconies overlooking a garden and small pool, in Fornells.
🔢 H2 ✉ Plaça S'Algaret 7, Fornells ☎ 971 376552 🕐 Mar–Oct

HOSTAL SA PRENSA

www.saprensa.com
Small, family-run hostel on the seafront at Ciutadella, with just eight rooms. Rooms at the front have terraces with sea views.
🔢 B4 ✉ Carrer Madrid 70, Ciutadella ☎ 971 382698 🕐 Mar–Oct

HOTEL MADRID

Small hotel near the seafront in Ciutadella, with 24 rooms and an outdoor pool.
🔢 B4 ✉ Carrer Madrid 60, Ciutadella ☎ 971 380328 🕐 May–Oct

MAR BLAVA

www.marblava.com
Old-style seaside hotel in a bright pink building in Ciutadella, with steps leading down to bathing platforms and views across the creek. 21 rooms.
🔢 B4 ✉ Avinguda del Mar 16, Ciutadella ☎ 971 380016 🕐 Apr–Oct

Mid-Range Hotels

PRICES

Expect to pay between €75 and €150 for a double room in mid-season (June and September).

BINIATRAM

www.biniatram.com
A 500-year-old farmhouse with its own private chapel, tennis court and swimming pool. There are walks in the gardens and a path through the estate leading to the sea. 11 rooms and apartments.
➕ B4 ✉ Carretera Cala Morell, Ciutadella ☎ 971 383113 ◐ All year

CASA ALBERTÍ

www.casalberti.com
An 18th-century townhouse in Maó's most elegant Georgian street. Six tasteful rooms, interior patio, roof terrace and comfy lounge with sofas, books and music.
➕ b2 ✉ Carrer d'Isabel II 9, Maó ☎ 971 354210 ◐ Mar–Oct

HESPERIA PATRICIA

www.hesperia.com
Conveniently situated between the old town and the port, this business hotel in Ciutadella has 44 rooms and an outdoor pool. The hotel is comfortable but perhaps somewhat lacking in character.
➕ B4 ✉ Passeig de Sant Nicolau 90-92, Ciutadella ☎ 971 385511 ◐ All year

HOTEL AGAMENÓN

www.sethotels.com
Seaside hotel at Es Castell, whose 75 rooms all have balconies overlooking Maó harbour. There is a large outdoor pool and a private dock for yachts.
➕ L7 ✉ Carrer Agamenón 16, Es Castell ☎ 971 362150 ◐ May–Oct

HOTEL AUDAX

www.rtmhotels.com
Hotel Audax is a large beach hotel at Cala Santa Galdana with 244 rooms. There is a spa and wellness centre featuring an indoor pool and treatments including hydromassage, chocolate therapy and seaweed wraps.
➕ D5 ✉ Cala Santa Galdana ☎ 971 154646 ◐ Apr–Oct

COLLINGWOOD HOUSE

Hotel del Almirante, also known as Collingwood House, was the home of Admiral Cuthbert Collingwood (1750–1810), a British navy officer who worked closely with Lord Nelson. The hotel has become a museum to the period of British rule in Menorca, with paintings and maps from the 18th century. Also on display are Talaiotic finds from Trepucó (▷ 38), discovered by archaeologist Margaret Murray during a stay here in 1934.

HOTEL CALA GALDANA

www.hotelcalagaldana.com
A large seaside hotel with 204 rooms at the heart of a busy resort. There are adult and children's pools, and the beach is a short walk away.
➕ D5 ✉ Cala Santa Galdana ☎ 971 154500 ◐ May–Oct

HOTEL CAPRI

www.rtmhotels.com
Comfortable city centre hotel in Maó, with a top-floor spa, rooftop pool and solarium with views over the city. 75 rooms.
➕ Off map at a2 ✉ Carrer Sant Esteve 8, Maó ☎ 971 361400 ◐ All year

HOTEL DEL ALMIRANTE

www.hoteldelalmirante.com
Historic hotel overlooking Maó harbour in a plum-red colonial villa, the former home of British Admiral Collingwood (▷ panel), and offering a pool, tennis court and garden terraces. 39 rooms.
➕ Off fold-out map at f4 ✉ Carretera Maó-Es Castell ☎ 971 362700 ◐ May–Oct

HOTEL PLATJA GRAN

www.grupoandria.com
Modern hotel in a prime position beside the beach at the start of the seafront promenade in Ciutadella. 46 rooms, most with balconies facing the sea.
➕ B4 ✉ Carrer Bisbe Juano 2, Ciutadella ☎ 971 480864 ◐ Feb–Dec

HOTEL PORT CIUTADELLA

www.sethotels.com

Stylish hotel on the seafront at Ciutadella, with rooms arranged around a central courtyard and pool. The spa centre features an indoor pool, jacuzzi, massage and beauty treatments. Some of the 94 rooms have sea-facing balconies.

➕ B4 ✉ Passeig Marítim 36, Ciutadella ☎ 971 482520 🕐 All year

HOTEL PORT MAHÓN

www.sethotels.com

Traditional luxury in an imposing colonial-style building overlooking the harbour at Maó, with steps leading down to the port. Popular with business visitors. 82 rooms.

➕ f3 (fold-out map) ✉ Avinguda Fort de l'Eau 13, Maó ☎ 971 362600 🕐 All year

HOTEL SA BARRERA

www.hotel-menorca.com

Elegant and romantic Italian-owned hotel on the cliffs at Cala En Porter, with a pool and views over the bay. Children under 12 are not accepted. 26 rooms.

➕ H7 ✉ Cala En Porter, Alaior ☎ 971 377126 🕐 May–Dec

HOTEL SAN MIGUEL

www.hotel-menorca.com

This former back-street hostel was restored by its Italian owners and opened in 2008 as Maó's first boutique hotel. The 16 suites combine classic style with modern design. There is also an attractive roof terrace for sun-bathing.

➕ c3 ✉ Carrer d'es Comerç 26, Maó ☎ 971 364059 🕐 All year

HOTEL SANTO TOMÀS

www.sethotels.com

Large seafront hotel on the beach at Sant Tomàs featuring an outdoor pool as well as spa facilities that include an indoor pool, jacuzzi, steam bath and massage. 85 rooms.

➕ F6 ✉ Platja Sant Tomàs ☎ 971 370025 🕐 May–Oct

LOAR

www.loarferreries.com

Loar is a three-star hotel facing the main square in Ferreries, with 20 rooms, 30 apartments and a rooftop jacuzzi, solarium and pool.

SPA HOTELS

Several hotels in Menorca have been developing spa and wellness centres in response to the growing demand for healthy holidays. Facilities include indoor pools, massage and beauty treatments ranging from seaweed therapy to Ayurvedic massage. Spa hotels include Hotel Audax at Cala Santa Galdana, Hotel Capri at Maó, Hotel Port Ciutadella and Hotel Santo Tomás and La Quinta at Cala En Bosc.

➕ F4 ✉ Avinguda Verge del Toro 2, Ferreries ☎ 971 374181 🕐 All year

SON TRETZE

www.hotelmenorca.com

An 18th-century house on the outskirts of Sant Lluís, with eight rooms and a small pool in the garden. The restaurant serves creative Mediterranean and African cuisine.

➕ L7 ✉ Camí de Binifadet 20, Sant Lluís ☎ 971 150943 🕐 All year

SON TRIAY NOU

www.sontriay.com

This striking pink colonial farmhouse off the road to Cala Santa Galdana was a pioneer of rural tourism in Menorca. With columns, arches and a double stairway leading to a private chapel, it makes an impressive sight. There are three rooms in the old house and a cottage in the gardens, as well as a swimming pool.

➕ D5 ✉ Carretera Cala Santa Galdana, km2.5 ☎ 971 155078 🕐 Apr–Oct

XUROY

www.xuroymenorca.com

Run by the same family since 1950, this delightfully old-fashioned beach hotel is situated beside the sea at Cala d'Alcaufar. 46 rooms.

➕ L8 ✉ Cala d'Alcaufar, Sant Lluís ☎ 971 151820 🕐 May–Oct

Luxury Hotels

PRICES

Expect to pay more than €150 for a double room in mid-season (June and September).

ALCAUFAR VELL

www.alcaufarvell.com
Country house near Sant Lluís dating back to the 14th century, with 10 rooms in the main house and 11 rooms in the converted stables and barns.
✚ L8 ✉ Carretera Cala d'Alcaufar, km8 ☎ 971 151874 ◷ Feb–Dec

BINIARROCA

www.biniarroca.com
Romantic hotel in a 16th-century farmhouse near Sant Lluís, that has been converted by an artist and an interior designer into an elegant child-free retreat, with 20 rooms in the house, gardens and cottages. Massage is offered under the poolside pergola in summer.
✚ L7 ✉ Camí Vell 57, Sant Lluís ☎ 971 150059 ◷ Apr–Nov

CA NA XINI

www.canaxini.com
The manor house at Hort de Sant Patrici (▷ 79) was opened in 2008 as a smart rural hotel, with eight rooms in contemporary style and a small pool in the gardens.
✚ F4 ✉ Camí de Sant Patrici s/n, Ferreries ☎ 971 373702 ◷ All year

HOTEL SANT IGNASI

www.santignasi.com
Rural hotel near Ciutadella, built in 1777 as the summer house of an aristocratic family. Twenty rooms decorated in 18th-century Anglo-Menorcan style and five suites in the old dairy.
✚ B4 ✉ Carretera Cala Morell s/n, Ciutadella ☎ 971 385575 ◷ 10 Jan–10 Dec

INSOTEL CLUB PUNTA PRIMA

www.insotelhotelgroup.com
A sprawling, upmarket family resort with 480 rooms in low-rise villas, set in extensive gardens with swimming pools and tennis courts close to the beach.
✚ L8 ✉ Carrer Migjera, Punta Prima ☎ 971 159200 ◷ May–Oct

MORVEDRA NOU

www.morvedranou.es
Rural hotel on the road to Cala Macarella, with 18 rooms in the 17th-century farmhouse and garden villas. The large garden has a pool and sea views.
✚ C4 ✉ Camí de Sant Joan de Missa, km7 ☎ 971 359521 ◷ Apr–Oct

LA QUINTA

www.laquintamenorca.com
This five-star spa hotel at Cala En Bosc is among the most exclusive in Menorca, with 82 rooms around the pool. Free minibus transfers to Ciutadella are offered.
✚ B5 ✉ Gran Via de Son Xoriguer s/n, Cala En Bosc ☎ 971 055000 ◷ May–Oct

SANT JOAN DE BINISSAIDA

www.binissaida.com
Rural hotel in an 18th-century farmhouse near the entrance to Maó harbour. There are six rooms in the main house and five in the old stables, all named after famous composers.
✚ L7 ✉ Camí de Binissaida 108, Es Castell ☎ 971 355598 ◷ Apr–Dec

SON GRANOT

www.songranot.com
An 18th-century Georgian mansion at Es Castell converted into a rural hotel with 10 rooms. The grounds include orchards, organic gardens, farm animals and a pool.
✚ L7 ✉ Carretera Sant Felip, Es Castell ☎ 971 355555 ◷ Mar–Dec

AGROTOURISM

Although most visitors to Menorca stay on the coast, some of the finest rooms can be found in the countryside. Some hotels, like Ca Na Xini, are situated on working farms, while others are rural hotels occupying old manor houses and farmhouses. What they all have in common are peaceful surroundings, locally produced food, and a satisfying combination of history, nature and modern comforts.

This section gives you all the practical information you need to help plan your visit and make the most of your time in Menorca. Use the Timeline to familiarize yourself with key moments and events from Menorcan and Spanish history.

Planning Ahead

When to Go

Almost all visitors to Menorca arrive between April and October, especially during the peak summer tourist season which lasts from mid-June to mid-September. Outside these times, the island is quiet, the beaches are deserted and many hotels and restaurants close their doors for the winter.

TIME

L Menorca is one hour ahead of the UK, in the same time zone as mainland Spain and most of continental Europe.

AVERAGE DAILY MAXIMUM TEMPERATURES

JAN	FEB	MAR	APR	MAY	JUN	JUL	AUG	SEP	OCT	NOV	DEC
14°C	15°C	17°C	19°C	22°C	26°C	29°C	29°C	27°C	23°C	18°C	15°C
57°F	59°F	63°F	66°F	72°F	79°F	84°F	84°F	81°F	73°F	64°F	59°F

Spring (March to May) is mild, with sunshine and showers. This is a good time for walking, cycling and golf.
Summer (June to August) is peak season, when prices and temperatures rise. The beaches are full and the island is geared up for tourists.
Autumn (September to November) is mild, and the sea is usually warm enough for swimming until the end of October.
Winter (December to February) can be wet and windy, but also has crisp, sunny days. Most hotels are closed, but Maó and Ciutadella remain lively.

WHAT'S ON

January *Festa de Sant Antoni* (16–17 Jan): Celebrations in Ciutadella and across the island on the anniversary of the conquest of Menorca from the Moors.
Cabalgata de los Reyes Magos (5–6 Jan): The Three Kings arrive in Maó harbour, parade through the streets, and throw sweets to the children to mark the end of Christmas and Twelfth Night.
February *Carnaval*: Fancy dress balls and parades during the days before Lent.
March/April *Setmana Santa*: Religious processions for Holy Week and Good Friday in Maó and Ciutadella.

June *Festa de Sant Joan* (23–24 Jun): The start of the fiesta season is marked by the island's biggest festival in Ciutadella, with horse riders in aristocratic costume representing the medieval religious brotherhoods of the nobility, peasants and clergy. It begins on the Sunday before 23 June with the Dia des Be, when a man dressed as John the Baptist carries a live lamb through the streets. On 23–24 June, horses rear and prance in Plaça des Born, there are equestrian games, fireworks and a horseback procession to Ermita de Sant Joan de Missa.

July–August Patron saints' feast days are celebrated with music, dancing and horsemanship in towns across the island, including Es Mercadal (third weekend in Jul), Es Castell (24–25 Jul), Alaior (first weekend after 10 Aug) and Ferreries (24–25 Aug).
Mare de Déu de Carme (16 Jul): The blessing of fishing boats in Maó, Ciutadella and Fornells in honour of the protector of fishermen.
September *Mare de Déu de Gràcia* (8 Sep): The climax of the fiesta season in Maó, with street parties, equestrian games and firework displays.

Menorca Online

www.spain.info
The Turespaña website has links to Spanish tourist office sites in 17 countries including the UK and US. Includes a trip planner, practical information and a diary of festivals and events.

www.illesbalears.es
Tourist information for the Balearic islands of Mallorca, Menorca, Ibiza and Formentera, including weather forecasts, event listings, and live beach reports.

www.emenorca.org
The official tourism site of the Menorca Island Council has background information on history, geology, fiestas, nature and the UNESCO Biosphere Reserve. It also has a complete database of the island's beaches and their facilities.

www.visitmenorca.com
The site of the Menorca Hotel Association allows you to search for accommodation by category and make online reservations for hotels, villas and apartments.

www.enmenorca.org
Site aimed at those who enjoy messing about on the water. Information on sailing, windsurfing, scuba diving, waterskiing, kayak, yacht and motorboat charter in Menorca, together with full lists of local operators. Other sports included are horse riding, cycling and golf.

www.menorcamonumental.org
Site listing all of Menorca's museums, ancient monuments and historic attractions which are open to visitors. Includes brief descriptions, contact information, opening times and prices.

www.menorca.info
Online digital edition of Menorca's daily newspaper, with articles in Spanish. Includes cultural agenda and lists of exhibitions and events. A few articles are published each week in English.

PRIME TRAVEL SITES

www.fodors.com
A complete travel planner. You can use the site to book flights, car rental and hotels, read articles by travel writers and ask questions to fellow travellers.

www.theaa.com
Travel and motoring advice from the Automobile Association. Includes route planning and driving laws for European countries.

INTERNET CAFÉS

Many hotels offer internet access, with a computer in the lobby which may be coin-operated or free to hotel guests. If you are taking your own laptop to Menorca, many hotels have wireless connections and modem points in the rooms. There are internet cafés in the main towns and resorts.

Ca N'Internet
www.caninternet.net
✉ Avinguda Mestre Garí 48, Es Mercadal
☎ 971 375359
🕐 Mon 5–10pm, Tue–Sat 11–2, 5–10
💶 €4 per hour

MenorKfoto
✉ Calle Miguel Sorá 2, Maó
☎ 971 365266
🕐 Mon–Sat 10–2, 5–9
💶 €4 per hour

Getting There

ENTRY REQUIREMENTS

● Visas are not required by citizens of the UK, US, Canada or EU countries, so you just need a valid passport to enter Spain. It is a legal requirement to keep your passport or national identity card with you at all times, and you will need to show it when you rent a car or book into hotels.

● Passengers on all flights to and from Spain are required to supply advance passenger information (API) to the Spanish authorities—full names, nationality, date of birth and travel document details, namely a passport number. This information is compulsory. Travel agents can collect this information at the time of booking, or you can give it to staff at check-in desks. Online, give the information at the time of booking.

INSURANCE

EU citizens receive free health care on production of their EHIC card, but private medical insurance is still advised and is essential for all other visitors. It is also a good idea to take out insurance cover for cancellation of your holiday and for loss or theft of money and valuables.

AIRPORTS

Menorca airport (☎ 971 157000; www.aena.es) is situated at Sant Climent, 5km (3 miles) from Maó. Facilities include tourist information, car hire, ATMs (cash machines), cafés and shops. The international airport code is MAH.

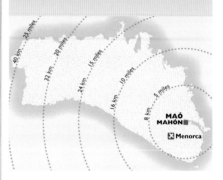

ARRIVING BY AIR

The growth of European budget airlines means that there is a wide range of flights to Menorca, particularly during the summer months. Tickets are priced according to demand, so it pays to shop around and the best deals are always available online.

● The Spanish national airline Iberia (www.iberia.com) has daily flights to Menorca throughout the year from Madrid and Palma de Mallorca, with connections to other Spanish and European cities.

● Budget airlines with flights from the Spanish mainland include Click Air (www.clickair.com) from Barcelona, Air Europa (www.aireuropa.com) and Spanair (www.spanair.com).

● From the UK, Easyjet (www.easyjet.com) flies to Menorca from Bristol, Liverpool, Newcastle and London Gatwick, and Monarch (www.monarch.co.uk) from Luton, Gatwick, Birmingham and Manchester.

● Air Berlin (www.airberlin.com) flies from Berlin, Munich and other German cities in summer, and also from Amsterdam, Copenhagen, Vienna and Zurich.

● There are numerous charter flights in summer from regional airports in the UK, Germany and Spain.

FROM THE AIRPORT
Buses leave the airport every 30 minutes throughout the day for the central bus station in Maó (€1.50). From November to April, the timetable is reduced to every 30 minutes from Monday to Friday and once an hour at weekends. The journey time is around 15 minutes. At the bus station, you can transfer to local buses for destinations in Maó and island-wide buses to Ciutadella and elsewhere. There is also a taxi rank in front of the airport terminal. A taxi from the airport costs around €10 to Maó and €50 to Ciutadella.

ARRIVING BY SEA
Car and passenger ferries to Menorca from the Spanish mainland operate throughout the year, with increased frequency in summer. The main route is Barcelona to Maó, with overnight car ferries (9 hours) operated by Baleària (☎ 902 160180; www.balearia.com), Iscomar (☎ 902 119128; www.iscomar.com) and Trasmediterránea (☎ 902 454645; www. trasmediterranea.es). Trasmediterránea also have a weekly departure from Valencia to Maó via Palma (14 hours). For inter-island travel, Iscomar operates daily car ferries from the port of Alcúdia in Mallorca to Ciutadella (2.5 hours), and Baleària has fast passenger ferries from Barcelona (4 hours) and Alcúdia (1 hour) to Ciutadella.

FROM THE PORT
The ferry terminals at Maó and Ciutadella are close to the city centres. In Maó, buses link the port with the central bus station every 30 minutes from Monday to Friday and once an hour at weekends. In Ciutadella, there are hourly buses from the ferry terminal to the city centre. Alternatively, you can always find a taxi to take you to your hotel.

TOURIST INFORMATION

● The tourist information office in the airport arrivals hall is open all year. You can pick up a map of the island and a weekly information sheet with details of markets, festivals and events.

● From November to April, tourist information is available from Fundació Destí Menorca, Cós de Gràcia 30, Maó.

● From May to October, there are seasonal tourist information offices in Maó at the bus station and beside the harbour at Moll de Llevant.

● The main tourist office in Ciutadella at Plaça de la Catedral is open throughout the year. There is also a seasonal office open from May to October inside the ferry terminal for passengers arriving by sea.

● Ciutadella has its own city tourist office at the town hall on Plaça des Born (Mon–Fri 9–2), and a summer information kiosk by the bus stop in Plaça dels Pins.

● The tourist office inside the harbourmaster's office at Fornells is open from May to October.

● Tourist information in Catalan, Spanish and English is available on a local rate information line (☎ 902 929015) from 10–6 daily throughout the year.

Getting Around

GETTING YOUR BEARINGS

Finding your way around Menorca by car is easy. A single main road runs across the island for 45km (28 miles) from Maó to Ciutadella, with a single lane in each direction. Apart from a few roads in the southeast, almost all other roads lead off the Me-1 to the north and south coasts.

CAR RENTAL AGENCIES

Avis
☎ 971 361576;
www.avis.es
Europcar
☎ 971 366400;
www.europcar.es
Hertz
☎ 971 354092;
www.hertz.es
National
☎ 971 366213;
www.atesa.es

BUSES

Buses across the island depart from the central bus station in Maó, behind the barracks in Plaça de S'Esplanada. The main routes operate throughout the year, with additional services to the beaches from May to October. There has been significant investment in public transport over the last few years and bus travel is efficient, reliable and cheap. A single fare from Maó to Ciutadella costs €4.40.

● Bus 1 runs from Maó to Ciutadella via Alaior, Es Mercadal and Ferreries, with hourly departures from Monday to Friday and a reduced service at weekends.
● Bus 14 is an express, non-stop service from Maó to Ciutadella up to 10 times a day from Monday to Friday.
● Other year-round services include Maó to Es Castell, Sant Lluís, Sant Climent, Es Migjorn Gran and Fornells.
● There are two circular routes in Maó linking the bus station, city centre and port, with departures every 30 minutes Monday to Friday and hourly at weekends.
● Buses from Ciutadella depart from the bus stops in Plaça dels Pins. Local buses include a shuttle from the city to the port, and buses to the nearby beach resorts of Cala En Blanes, Cala Blanca and Cala En Bosc.
● Services in summer include Maó to Son Bou, Ferreries to Cala Santa Galdana, Ciutadella to Sant Tomàs, Es Mercadal to Fornells and Es Migjorn Gran to Es Mercadal and Cala Tomàs.
● The Bus Nit (night bus) runs on Friday and Saturday nights from Sant Lluís to Ciutadella via Es Castell, Maó, Alaior, Es Mercadal and Ferreries. Departures from Sant Lluís and Ciutadella are at midnight and 3am on Friday (Saturday morning) and 11pm, 1am, 3am and 5am on Saturday (Sunday morning).

DRIVING

Although buses provide an efficient service between main towns and coastal resorts, to get

the most out of a visit to Menorca you really need a car. Driving allows you to reach those out-of-the-way beaches and monuments which are in many ways the essence of Menorca. The easiest way to hire a car is to book in advance through one of the international car rental agencies with offices at the airport (▷ panel opposite). If you only need a car for a few days, you can arrange it through your hotel or agencies in your resort. There is a 24-hour fuel station on the ring road at Maó, and other fuel stations at the airport, Sant Lluís and along the main road from Maó to Ciutadella. There is also a fuel station on the road from Maó to Fornells.

CAR HIRE

To hire a car, you must be over 21 and you will need a passport, driving licence and credit card. Keep your passport, driving licence and car hire documents with you at all times (never leave these unattended in the car). Check the insurance details. Most policies require you to pay a hefty excess in the event of an accident, though this can usually be waived for an additional premium. Contact your car hire company immediately in the event of an accident or breakdown.

CYCLING

Menorca has over 200km (125 miles) of bicycle routes and more are being developed all the time. They include a trail across the island from Ciutadella to Sant Lluís, which follows minor roads and tracks for 66km (41 miles). You can hire bicycles from some hotels, campsites and Velos Joan in Ciutadella (▷ 102).

TAXIS

Taxis can be hired from taxi ranks at Plaça de S'Esplanada in Maó and Plaça dels Pins in Ciutadella. Fares are reasonable and fixed, though you should check with the driver in advance. Radio taxis can be booked 24 hours a day by calling ☎ 971 367111 in Maó or ☎ 971 382896 in Ciutadella. You can also book a taxi through your hotel.

RULES OF THE ROAD

● The speed limit is 90kph (56mph) on the Maó to Ciutadella road and 50kph (31mph) on all other roads, unless otherwise indicated.
● The drink-drive limit is 0.05 per cent and is strictly enforced. Never drive under the influence of alcohol.
● Seat belts must be worn at all times.
● Children under 12 and less than 135cm (4ft 6in) tall must use a child restraint system adapted to their size and weight.
● Pay-and-display car parking spaces are indicated by blue lines. During working hours, you must buy a ticket and display it in your windscreen.

VISITORS WITH DISABILITIES

Buses from Maó to Ciutadella are adapted for disabled passengers and more buses are likely to be made accessible to wheelchairs over the next few years. Most hotels and public buildings have disabled access, but access to remote beaches and archaeological sites is limited.

Essential Facts

EMERGENCY NUMBERS

● The emergency telephone number is 112 for police, ambulance and fire brigade.

CONSULATES

● France ☎ 971 354387
● Germany ☎ 971 361668
● UK ☎ 971 367818

MONEY

● The euro is the official currency of Spain.
● Credit and debit cards are widely accepted, and can also be used for withdrawing cash from ATMs (cash machines), which usually offer on-screen instructions in several languages.

5 euros

10 euros

50 euros

100 euros

ELECTRICITY

● The power supply is 220V. Sockets take two round pins, so take an adaptor if necessary.

ETIQUETTE

● It is polite to shake hands on greeting. The usual greeting between friends of the opposite sex is a kiss on both cheeks.
● Topless sunbathing is acceptable at beaches and hotel pools but you should cover up elsewhere and you should not walk around towns and cities in a bikini or swimming costume.
● Modest dress is essential for both sexes when visiting churches.
● Tipping is a fact of life in Spain. Add up to 10 per cent of the bill in restaurants, and leave some small change in bars. Taxi drivers, hotel staff and tour guides all appreciate a tip.

MEDICAL TREATMENT

● EU citizens receive free health care on production of their EHIC card, but private medical insurance is still advised and is essential for all other visitors.
● The main hospital is Hospital Mateu Orfila, on the ring road in Maó (☎ 971 487000).
● Prescription and non-prescription medicines are available from pharmacies, which have a flashing green cross above the door. Outside normal hours, a notice on the door of each pharmacy tells you the address of the nearest duty chemist.

NEWSPAPERS

● *Menorca* is a daily newspaper in Catalan and Spanish, with a supplement in English on Tuesdays.
● *Ultima Hora* is a daily newspaper published in Mallorca with a separate edition for Menorca.
● Foreign newspapers are often available on the day of publication.

OPENING HOURS

● Banks: Mon–Sat 8–2.
● Shops: Mon–Sat 9–1, 4–8. Some shops close

on Saturday afternoons, while supermarkets and shops in the beach resorts tend to stay open throughout the day.

PLACES OF WORSHIP

● There are Roman Catholic churches in every town and village and a cathedral in Ciutadella.

● The Anglican church in Es Castell has Holy Communion on Wednesday at 11am, and Sunday at 9am and 11am (✉ Carrer Stuart 20, Es Castell ☎ 971 352378; www.anglicanchurchinmenorca.org).

POST OFFICES

● The main post office is at Carrer Bonaire 15, Maó. There is another main post office on Plaça des Born, Ciutadella. Both are open Monday to Friday 8.30am–8.30pm and Saturday 9.30–1.

● The post offices at Alaior, Es Mercadal, Es Castell and Sant Lluís are open Monday to Friday 8.30–2.30 and Saturday 9.30–1.

● Stamps can also be bought from tobacconists and shops selling postcards.

● Sending a postcard to Europe costs €0.60.

TELEPHONES

● To use a public telephone, buy a *tarjeta telefónica* (phonecard), available for €6 and €12 from post offices, news kiosks and tobacconists. Insert your card and follow the instructions on the screen.

● For calls within Menorca, dial the full nine-figure number including the local code 971.

● To call the UK, dial 00 44 followed by the local number, omitting the initial 0 from the area code. For calls to other countries, dial 00 followed by the country code.

● The telephone in your hotel room is likely to be expensive, especially for international calls.

● Most European mobile phones work well in Menorca. You may need to contact your network provider before you go to check that international roaming is set up on your account. For extended stays , it may be cheaper to buy a Spanish SIM card and insert it into your phone.

PUBLIC HOLIDAYS

● **1 January:** New Year's Day
● **6 January:** Epiphany
● **March/April:** Maundy Thursday, Good Friday, Easter Monday
● **1 May:** Labour Day
● **15 August:** Assumption of the Virgin
● **12 October:** Spanish National Day
● **1 November:** All Saints' Day
● **6 December:** Constitution Day
● **8 December:** Feast of the Immaculate Conception
● **25–26 December:** Christmas

SENSIBLE PRECAUTIONS

● Leave cash and valuables in a hotel safe; do not carry more cash than you need.
● Do not leave valuable items unattended on the beach while you swim.
● Beware of pickpockets in crowded places.
● Never leave items visible inside your car; lock them out of sight in the boot.
● Keep a photocopy of your passport and other important documents in your hotel room.
● Pay attention to safety flags on the beach, and never swim in the sea when the red flag is flying.
● Do not swim after drinking alcohol.

Language

The official languages of the Balearic islands are Catalan and Castilian Spanish. Most people in Menorca are bilingual, speaking both languages fluently, and many people speak English as well. During the Franco dictatorship, the Castilian language was imposed across Spain and regional languages such as Catalan were forbidden. Since 1983, there has been a revival of Catalan and its local dialect Menorquín, particularly in place names which are given in Catalan throughout this book. Although Catalan is the language of everyday conversation in Menorca, Spanish is universally understood and a knowledge of Spanish will get you by.

Spanish

BASIC VOCABULARY	
good morning	*buenos dias*
good afternoon/ evening	*buenas tardes*
good night	*buenas noches*
hello (informal)	*hola*
goodbye (informal)	*hasta luego/hasta pronto*
hello (on the phone)	*¿Diga?*
goodbye	*adios*
please	*por favor*
thank you	*gracias*
you're welcome	*de nada*
how are you? (formal)	*¿Cómo está?*
how are you? (informal)	*¿Que tal?*
I'm fine	*estoy bien*
I'm sorry	*lo siento*
excuse me	*perdón*
I don't understand	*no entiendo*
I don't speak Spanish	*no hablo español*
how much is it?	*¿cuanto es?*
where is the...?	*¿dónde está...?*
do you have...?	*¿tiene...?*
I'd like...	*me gustaría*
I don't know	*No lo sé*
It doesn't matter	*No importa*
How much/many?	*¿Cuánto/cuántos?*
Is/are there?	*¿Hay?*

USEFUL WORDS	
yes	*sí*
no	*no*
Where?	*¿Dónde?*
When?	*¿Cuándo?*
Why?	*¿Por qué?*
What?	*¿Que?*
Who?	*¿Quién?*
How?	*¿Cómo?*
ticket	*entrada*
big	*grande*
small	*pequeño*
with	*con*
without	*sin*
hot	*caliente*
cold	*frío*
early	*temprano*
late	*tarde*
here	*aquí*
there	*alli*
today	*hoy*
tomorrow	*mañana*
yesterday	*ayer*
menu	*la carta*
entrance	*entrada*
exit	*salida*
open	*abierto*
closed	*cerrado*
good	*bueno*
bad	*malo*

Catalan

BASIC VOCABULARY

yes/no	si/no
please	per favor
thank you	gràcies
welcome	de res
hello	hola
goodbye	adéu
good morning	bon dia
good afternoon	bona tarda
goodnight	bona nit
excuse me	perdoni
you're welcome	de res
how are you?	com va?
do you speak English?	parla anglès?
I don't understand	no ho entenc
today	avui
tomorrow	demà

MONEY

how much?	quant es?
bank	banc
exchange office	oficina de canvi
coin	moneda
change	camvi
banknote	bitllet de banc
cheque	xec
traveller's cheque	xec de viatge
credit card	carta de crèdit
exchange rate	tant per cent
commission charge	comissió

TRANSPORTATION

how do I get to...?	per anar a...?
single ticket	senzill-a
return ticket	anar i tornar
aeroplane/airport	avió/aeroport
train	tren
bus	autobús
car	cotxe

HOTELS

hotel	hotel
bed and breakfast	llit i berenar
single room	habitació senzilla
double room	habitació doble
one person	una persona
one night	una nit
reservation	reservas
room service	servei d'habitació
bath	bany
shower	dutxa
toilet	toaleta
key	clau
lift	ascensor
balcony	balcó
sea view	vista al mar

EATING OUT

open	obert
closed	tancat
café	cafè
pub/bar	celler
breakfast	berenar
lunch	dinar
dinner	sopar
waiter	cambrer
waitress	cambrera
starter	primer plat
main course	segón plat
dessert	postres
bill	cuenta
beer	cervesa
wine	vi
water	aigua

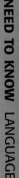

Timeline

THE YOUNG CONQUERER

Alfons III of Aragón (1265–91) was only 21 when he captured Menorca from the Moors in 1287. Although he spent just 45 days on the island, his visit changed the course of history by establishing the Catalan language and culture in Menorca.

POUR ENCOURAGER LES AUTRES

Admiral John Byng (1704–57) became the first British admiral to be executed, after being found guilty of neglect by court-martial following the loss of Menorca to the French. French author Voltaire immortalized the episode in *Candide*: 'In this country it is thought good to kill an admiral from time to time to encourage the others.'

Left to right: Martello tower near Cala d'Alcaufar; the British Admiral John Byng (1704–57); painted houses in Maó; a stone cross; carving on the cliff at Cales Coves; Byzantine mosaic from the basilica of Es Fornàs de Torelló

2000–123BC The Talaiotic period produces burial caves, *navetas*, *talaiots* and *taulas*.

123BC Roman conquest. Menorca is named Balearis Minor. The first towns are established at Maó and Ciutadella.

AD902 Arab conquest. The Balearic islands enter the emirate of Córdoba. Ciutadella becomes Medina Minurka.

1287 Conquest by Alfons III of Aragón. After his death, Mallorca rules Menorca. Catalan becomes the main language.

1349 The Balearics are incorporated into Catalonia and Aragón.

1492 Aragón unites with Castile and Granada to create modern Spain.

1535–58 Maó and Ciutadella are destroyed by Turkish pirates.

1708 British troops occupy Menorca in the name of Charles, Archduke of Austria.

1713 The Treaty of Utrecht confirms British rule. Sir Richard Kane becomes governor and moves the capital to Maó.

1756 The Battle of Menorca results in a French victory and the execution of British Naval officer Admiral Byng in 1757.

1763–82 Second British occupation.

1782–98 Menorca returns to Spanish rule.

1798–1802 Final British occupation. The Treaty of Amiens returns Menorca to Spain.

1909 Formation of a Society for the Attraction of Foreigners.

1936–39 Spanish Civil War. Menorca remains Republican and is the last part of Spain to surrender to General Franco.

1939–75 Dictatorship under Franco. The Catalan language is banned. Tourism becomes a significant industry.

1975 Death of Franco and restoration of the monarchy.

1983 The Balearic Islands becomes an autonomous region, with Catalan as an official language.

1986 Spain joins the European Community.

1993 Menorca is designated a UNESCO Biosphere Reserve.

2002 Visitor numbers reach 1 million.

2008 Menorca announces plans to bid for the International Island Games in 2017.

THE RISE AND RISE OF TOURISM

Back in 1950, there were just 200 hotel rooms in Menorca. The opening of the new airport in 1969 unleashed a tourism boom, with high-rise hotels appearing on the coast and visitor numbers doubling almost overnight. By 2002, Menorca was receiving 1 million foreign tourists a year and the Balearic government introduced an eco-tax on visitors of €1 per day. The tax was abandoned following protests in 2003.

THE WORLD'S OLDEST MAN

Joan Riudavets Moll (1889–2004) from Es Migjorn Gran was officially the world's oldest man when he died at the age of 114. Shortly before his death, he said that his biggest regret was not meeting his mother, who died when he was just 15 days old. His younger brother Josep celebrated his 100th birthday in 2007.

NEED TO KNOW TIMELINE

Index

TWINPACK
Menorca

WRITTEN BY Tony Kelly
VERIFIED BY Mona Kraus and Lindsay Bennett
COVER DESIGN Jacqueline Bailey
DESIGN WORK Jacqueline Bailey and Maggie Aldred
INDEXER Marie Lorimer
IMAGE RETOUCHING AND REPRO Sarah Montgomery, Michael Moody and James Tims
PROJECT EDITOR Kim Lehoucka
SERIES EDITOR Cathy Harrison

© AA MEDIA LIMITED 2010

Colour separation by AA Digital Department
Printed and bound by Leo Paper Products, China

A CIP catalogue record for this book is available from the British Library.

ISBN 978-0-7495-6154-3

Published by AA Publishing, a trading name of AA Media Limited, whose registered office is Fanum House, Basing View, Basingstoke, Hampshire RG21 4EA. Registered number 06112600.

Front cover image: AA/J Tims
Back cover images: (i) AA/J Tims; (ii) AA/C Sawyer; (iii) AA/P Baker; (iv) AA/J Tims

A03639
Maps in this title produced from mapping © KOMPASS GmbH, A-6063 Rum, Innsbruck

The Automobile Association would like to thank the following photographers, companies and picture libraries for their assistance in the preparation of this book.

Abbreviations for the pictures credits are as follows – (t) top; (b) bottom; (c) centre; (l) left; (r) right; (AA) AA World Travel Library.

1 AA/J Tims; **2–18 top panel** AA/J Tims; 4 AA/J Tims; 5 AA/J Tims; **6tl** AA/J Tims; **6tc** AA/C Sawyer; **6tr** AA/J Tims; **6bl** AA/J Tims; **6bc** AA/J Tims; **6br** AA/J Tims; **7tl** AA/J Tims; **7tc** AA/J Tims; **7tr** AA/J Tims; **7bl** AA/J Tims; **7bc** AA/J Tims; **7br** AA/J Tims; **10t** AA/J Tims; **10c(i)** AA/J Tims; **10c(ii)** AA/J Tims; **10/11b** AA/J Tims; **11t(i)** AA/J Tims; **11t(ii)** AA/J Tims; **11c(i)** AA/J Tims; **11c(ii)** AA/J Tims; **12t** AA/J Tims ; **12c(i)** AA/J Tims; **12c(ii)** AA/C Sawyer; **12b** AA/C Sawyer; **13t** AA/C Sawyer; **13t(i)** AA/ A Mockford & Nick Bonetti; **13c** Brand X Pics; **13b** Digitalvision; **14t** AA/C Sawyer; **14c(i)** AA/M Chaplow; **14c(ii)** AA/M Chaplow; **14b** AA/J Tims; **15** AA/C Sawyer; **16t** AA/J Tims; **16c(i)** AA/J Tims; **16c(ii)** AA/ C Sawyer; **16b** AA/J Tims; **17t** Digitalvision; **17c(i)** Imagestate; **17c(ii)** AA/C Sawyer; **17b** AA/J Tims; **18t** AA/J Tims; **18c(i)** AA/J Tims; **18c(ii)** AA/J Tims; **18b** AA/ J Tims; **19t** AA/J Tims; **19c(i)** AA/J Tims; **19c(ii)** AA/J Tims; **19b** AA/J Tims; **20/21** AA/J Tims; **24t** AA/J Tims; **24b** AA/J Tims; **25** AA/J Tims; **26l** Courtesy of La Mola Fortalesa Isabel II Mao-Menorca; **26/27t** Courtesy of La Mola Fortalesa Isabel II Mao-Menorca; **26/27b** Courtesy of La Mola Fortalesa Isabel II Mao-Menorca; **27r** Courtesy of La Mola Fortalesa Isabel II Mao-Menorca; **28** Courtesy of the Consell Insular de Menorca; **29** Courtesy of the Consell Insular de Menorca; **30** AA/J Tims; **31t** AA/J Tims; **31b** AA/J Tims; **32l** AA/J Tims; **32r** AA/J Tims; **34l** Courtesy of the Teatre de Mao; **34r** Courtesy of the Teatre de Mao; **35–38 top panel** AA/J Tims; **35l** AA/J Tims; **35r** AA/J Tims; **36l** AA/J Tims; **36r** AA/J Tims; **37l** AA/J Tims; **37r** AA/J Tims; **38l** AA/J Tims; **38r** AA/J Tims; **39** AA/J Tims; **40** AA/S McBride; **41** AA/ J Tims; **42** AA/J Tims; **43–44** AA/C Sawyer; **45** AA/J Tims; **48l** AA/J Tims; **48r** AA/ J Tims; **49l** AA/J Tims; **49r** AA/J Tims; **50** AA/J Tims; **51** AA/J Tims; **52** AA/J Tims; **53** AA/J Tims; **54l** AA/J Tims; **54tr** AA/J Tims; **54br** AA/J Tims; **55t** AA/J Tims; **55bl** AA/J Tims; **55br** AA/J Tims; **56/57** AA/J Tims; **57** AA/J Tims; **58l** AA/J Tims; **58r** AA/ J Tims; **59l** AA/J Tims; **59r** AA/J Tims; **60/61** AA/J Tims; **61** AA/J Tims; **62–64 top panel** AA/J Tims; **62l** AA/J Tims; **62r** AA/J Tims; **63l** AA/J Tims; **63r** AA/J Tims; **64l** Geoff Williamson SuperPrime/Alamy; **64r** AA/J Tims; **65** AA/J Tims; **66** AA/ J Tims; **67t** AA/S McBride; **67b** AA/C Sawyer; **68** AA/C Sawyer; **69** AA/J Tims; **72l** AA/J Tims; **72r** AA/J Tims; **73l** AA/J Tims; **73r** AA/J Tims; **74** AA/J Tims; **75** AA/ J Tims; **76** AA/J Tims; **76/77** AA/J Tims; **77** AA/J Tims; **78l** AA/J Tims; **78r** AA/ J Tims; **79l** Jordi Escandell/Hort de Sant Patrici SL; **79r** Hort de Sant Patrici SL; **80–82 top panel** AA/J Tims; **80l** AA/J Tims; **80r** AA/J Tims; **81l** AA/J Tims; **81r** AA/J Tims; **82l** AA/J Tims; **82r** AA/J Tims; **83** AA/J Tims; **84t** AA/S McBride; **84b** AA/C Sawyer; **85** AA/J Tims; **86** AA/C Sawyer; **87** AA/J Tims; **90l** AA/J Tims; **90tr** AA/J Tims; **90br** AA/J Tims; **91t** AA/J Tims; **91bl** AA/J Tims; **91br** AA/J Tims; **92** AA/J Tims; **93** AA/J Tims; **94t** Courtesy of Lithica; **94bl** Courtesy of Lithica; **94/95** Courtesy of Lithica; **95** AA/J Tims; **96l** AA/J Tims; **96r** AA/J Tims; **97–100 top panel** AA/J Tims; **97l** Courtesy of the Casa Museu Pintor Torrent; **97r** AA/J Tims; **98l** AA/J Tims; **98r** AA/J Tims; **99l** AA/J Tims; **99r** AA/J Tims; **100l** AA/J Tims; **100r** AA/J Tims; **101** AA/J Tims; **102** AA/S McBride; **103** AA/ C Sawyer; **104** AA/C Sawyer; **105–106** AA/C Sawyer; **107** AA/J Tims; **108–112 top panel** AA/C Sawyer; **108t** AA/J Tims; **108c(i)** AA/J Tims; **108c(ii)** Stockbyte Royalty Free; **108b** AA/J Tims; **113** AA/J Tims; **114–125 top panel** AA/J Tims; **120** MRI Bankers Guide to Foreign Currency, Houston, USA; **124l** AA/J Tims; **124c** Mary Evans Picture Library; **124r** AA/J Tims; **125l** AA/W Voysey; **125c** AA/J Tims; **125r** AA/J Tims.

Every effort has been made to trace the copyright holders, and we apologise in advance for any accidental errors. We would be happy to apply any corrections in the following edition of this publication.